THE ART OF MAKING
WINE
AND LIQUEURS

THE ART OF MAKING

AND LIQUEURS

Betty Sampson

WITH ILLUSTRATIONS BY
ROSANNE SANDERS

AURUM PRESS

To my husband for his
encouragement and support

First published in hardback 1982 by Aurum Press Ltd
7 Greenland Street, London NW1 0ND
Paperback edition published 1987
This revised edition published 2002

A catalogue record for this book is available from the British Library

ISBN 978 1 85410 844 9

5 7 9 8 6 4
2009

Printed and bound in Great Britain by MPG Books Ltd, Bodmin

CONTENTS

FOREWORD

MY FIRST ACQUAINTANCE with Betty Sampson was in the early seventies, when she was Secretary of the Kingsbridge Wine Circle. She was then already an established winemaker and later became an exhibitor of some distinction, subsequently qualifying as a wine judge.

In 1977, with the assistance of her husband and family, they established an extensive commercial vineyard in South Devon, which they operated for the next twenty years. With such a wealth of practical experience, it seems a natural progression for her to have written a book on winemaking.

All good wine has a certain balance. On reading the manuscript of this book it was immediately apparent to me that such a balance had also been achieved in putting the basic facts to beginners in simple terms, yet at the same time presenting enough technical content to satisfy the particular needs of established winemakers and exhibitors.

The recipe section is a masterpiece of application to the art of winemaking, and this revised edition has been extended to cover liqueurs. Over a period of two years each recipe has been thoroughly tested to the author's own exacting standards before being included.

Betty Sampson brings to the following pages a breath of countryside, and blends it nicely with the science of winemaking. The result is unique. This superbly illustrated book is easy to understand, and will for many years meet the needs of new and old exponents of this absorbing pastime.

Peter K. Ineson
Convenor of Judges,
South West Counties Wine and Beermakers Federation

ᴑ𝒩TRODUCTION

WINE THROUGHOUT THE CENTURIES has been acclaimed for its beneficial qualities. In biblical times it was more wholesome to drink than water, and at festivities it helped to break down inhibitions, creating a relaxed and happy atmosphere. In present times a glass of wine gives a sense of expectation and will give pleasure and enhance even the most mundane meal.

Winemaking skills have passed from one generation to another, but it has always been associated with congenial gatherings of family and friends or an accompaniment to meals, enhancing and enriching them. We are fortunate in this new century not only to have the knowledge laid down by our forefathers, but also to be able to reap the benefits of technology of our present age.

Appreciation of wine, as in any other creative art, has a learning curve to be experienced. During the Depression of the 1930s and during World War II, very little wine was available; a generation elapsed without any wine appreciation. As wines again began to be imported, a slightly sweeter white wine was most people's choice and the less complex and flowery German wines gained popularity. Gradually more distinctive drier wines from the Moselle, Alsace and Chablis were preferred. The complexity of wines from South America, South Africa, the fresh clean New Zealand and English wines and the softer Australian ones are all gradually being appreciated. From Oregon State to California, the wines vary in style and complexity, and it is our privilege to evaluate them on their merit.

The progression of learning also applies to the reds, not to compare one against the other but to appreciate their own individual characteristics; some will prefer the rich red Burgundies, others the more acid and tannic wines of Bordeaux. Red wines are always drunk too quickly and before they have reached their full potential. Why not occasionally buy a good red Bordeaux and lay it down for 10 years, then you will be able to appreciate the velvety smoothness and complexity of a truly great red wine. This applies to home-made reds too: if only they can be laid down for a few years, their quality will be greatly enhanced.

Techniques in home-made winemaking have changed beyond recognition, and a variety of utensils has been designed to meet the demands of the amateur. Increased knowledge of the process of fermentation and the prevention of bacterial damage by careful use of additives has enabled winemakers to reach far higher standards of excellence than ever before.

My first venture into winemaking was in 1960 when my Devon garden produced an abundance of fruits which I could not utilise. Following this I helped in the formation of a local Wine Circle, of which I became an active member. The help and encouragement received from other members has been invaluable, and I have enjoyed the challenge of entering competitions

at local, county and
national level. Winning
prizes is rewarding and
provides the motivation
towards greater achievements, but losing concentrates
thoughtful attention to the problems and creates a desire to
get things right. I have experienced both, and I am grateful to show organis-
ers who have given myself and other winemakers the opportunities of trying
out our skills in competition. The general improvement in the quality of
home-made wines can be partly attributed to this competitive spirit.

In most wine-producing countries the definition of wine is 'the product
of the fermented juice of ripe grapes', but in cooler, more temperate climates
this definition may be extended to include 'a similar liquor made from other
fruits, juices, grains and flowers'. The grape is the perfect medium for winemaking in normal seasons, as it contains the correct amount of sugars, acids,
tannins, minerals and vitamins, and this allows the yeast to ferment actively,
converting the sugars to alcohol and carbon dioxide. In making country
wines it is possible to come close to this special quality imparted by the grape.
Acid, alcohol, aroma, body, flavour, texture and residual sugar all need to be
balanced, whether the wine is dry, medium-dry or dessert. In order to obtain
such a balance, careful selection of ingredients is essential: the best wines are
made when the sugars, acids and tannins in the fruit are at the correct levels
and no additions or subtractions are required.

This perfect balance is the foundation stone of successful winemaking.
Home winemakers often use only one type of fruit or vegetable, thereby
giving to the wine the predominant character of that particular ingredient.
Some will be high in acid or tannin and impart a strong flavour but will
lack body and texture; to others the opposite will apply. A wine made from
elderberries, for example, will contain a high proportion of flavour and tannin but will be lacking in acidity and body. Wines made primarily from
bananas, pears or parsnips will have more body but will be lacking in interest and flavour owing to their low acidity. Many winemakers try to correct
this imbalance by blending their wines together; my aim in the following
recipes has been to achieve the correct balance at a much earlier stage – by
the careful selection of ingredients which complement each other.

The recipes I have devised for this book have all been tested and have
consistently proved successful. They include flower, fruit, vegetable,

2

sparkling and dessert wines, plus a section on organic wines; and liqueurs, cocktails, long drinks, punches, non-alcoholic cups, mulled wines and coffees. The basic principles of winemaking are explained for the beginner, and there is a section devoted to fermentation, clearing, racking and some of the problems which may be encountered. Although I have attempted to keep all the instructions as straightforward as possible, the use of some technical terms is unavoidable. A simple explanation of these may be found in the Glossary on page 147, and once the basic principles are understood, the terms should present no problems.

A section has been included on viticulture in the UK, as many winemakers are now growing a few wine variety vines in their garden to produce their own special vintage. In the early 1970s I was motivated to plant 60 vines in the garden and this eventually lead in 1977 to the planting by my family of a four-acre vineyard. The 5000 vines planted were mainly of German origin. The acreage increased to 10 acres by 1980, with a business producing 20,000 to 30,000 bottles of wine a year, and we were able to welcome visitors from many parts of the world who were amazed at the quality of English wine. This commercial venture was enhanced by knowledge gained as an amateur winemaker; likewise, the experience gained in the commercial production of wine has enabled me to understand the principles of producing a balanced wine from garden fruits. Similarly, the production of home-made liqueurs has given an incentive to use summer fruits in making simple liqueurs which capture the true flavours of our fresh fruits.

I hope that this book will inspire those who have never made their own wine to begin; others who have never gone beyond the first stages will perhaps be encouraged to experiment and develop their own recipes. It will give an interest and knowledge to wine lovers, too, in the production of commercial and country wines, enabling them to appreciate and understand the complex and fascinating developments by the phenomenal ability of yeasts to turn fruits into classic vintages.

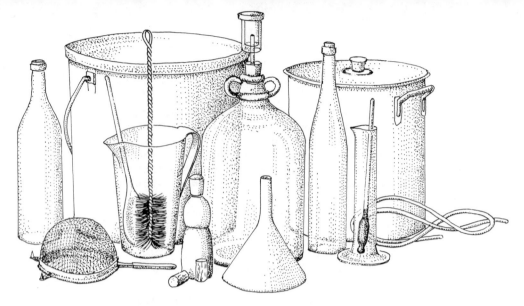

QUIPMENT

Although some kitchen utensils may be used to start with, certain basic equipment will have to be purchased. This can be obtained from home brew shops, which now often carry a wide selection. A very simple 'Beginner's Kit' is given on page 40, but for anyone at all serious about making wine, the following equipment will be needed:

Utensils
10-litre plastic bucket with lid
Nylon sieve
Straining bags
Plastic funnel (15cm/6-in. diameter)
Pyrex or plastic measuring jug
Large saucepan (preferably stainless steel)
Plastic siphon tubing (2m/6ft)
Bottle brush
Fermentation bungs and airlocks
Two 4.5-litre (1 gallon) demijohns
Hand corker and corks
Hydrometer and jar
Long-handled wooden or plastic spoon
Bottles (these can often be obtained from friends and hotels)

Chemicals
Sodium metabisulphite or Campden tablets
Pectin-destroying enzyme (liquid or powder form)
Yeast nutrients (ammonium phosphate, ammonium sulphate, magnesium sulphate)
Vitamin B_1 tablets
Grape tannin or tannic acid (powder or liquid form)
Acid, preferably combined tartaric, malic and citric mixture

Utensils

The golden rule is never to use equipment made of any metal other than stainless steel. As this is expensive, most items are made in white plastic, with the exception of saucepans. A few recipes advocate heating the ingredients using a stainless steel saucepan; if this type of pan is not available, use a good quality saucepan and as soon as the required heat has been obtained, remove the liquid to another container. The contents should never be allowed to stand in the vessel for any length of time. Wood is acceptable provided that it is kept scrupulously clean.

Plastic bucket with lid

It is essential for the plastic bucket or bin to have a tightly fitting lid. The size of the bucket will depend on the quantities you intend to make; if you are starting with very small quantities, a gallon ice-cream container will suffice for a while.

Straining bags

As most of the ingredients will be infused in water for short periods or fermented on the pulp, it is useful to have several straining bags. These may be purchased but the best and cheapest method is to make them yourself from remnants of nylon curtain material (select a firm net which has a fine mesh). The bags should be at least 40 x 35cm (16 x 14in.) for a 5-litre bucket and 50 x 43cm (20 x 17in.) for a 10-litre bucket.

It is a good idea, and essential for the larger sizes, to have two bags, one inside the other, to withstand the weight of pulp. This will also give a clearer juice, as less pulp debris will escape into the receiving container. Do not make the bags with double net, as small pieces of debris will become trapped between the layers, making it very difficult to clean them.

Airlocks

An airlock is necessary to exclude the air from the fermenting must while allowing the carbon dioxide to escape. The water level in the airlock should be about 1.2cm ($^1/_2$ in.) and contain a little sulphite solution. Simple plastic ones are readily available, which are fitted into the bored rubber bung.

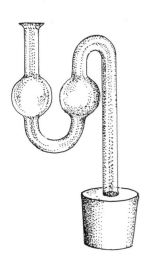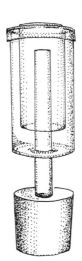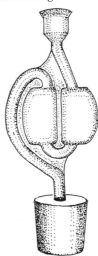

Demijohns

For most winemakers the glass demijohn is the best storage vessel, as it is easy to handle and clean. Large glass containers are now more readily obtainable, and provided that enough storage space is available, they are ideal for quantities of up to 25 litres (5½ gal.). Plastic containers are not suitable for long storage periods, as they frequently impart a plastic taint to the wine.

Hydrometer

Sooner or later the winemaker will have to become acquainted with a hydrometer. This is an instrument for measuring the specific gravity (SG) of a liquid compared with that of water, and although it may appear complicated, it is, in fact, very simple to use. A hydrometer is invaluable in winemaking to estimate the quantity of sugar in the fruit juice so that calculations can then be made on the extra quantity of sugar needed to obtain the required alcoholic strength. The hydrometer can also be used as a guide to progress during fermentation and to ascertain when it is completed.

When making pure grape juice wines, wine from kits and other extracted fruit juices, or after straining the liquid from fruits infused in cold water or pasteurisation, an exact calculation can be made of the potential alcoholic strength of the finished wines by taking a hydrometer reading before adding the yeasts.

With fermentations on the pulp, however, hydrometer readings will give only a rough guide, as even if the reading is taken from some of the strained liquid before the yeast is added, there will still be a considerable amount of sugar retained in the fruit pulp, which will not be fully extracted until the yeast enzymes have finished their work.

Chemicals

Sodium or potassium metabisulphite (Campden tablets) have two important roles, one as a sterilising agent for equipment and the other to sterilise the prepared fruit ('must') and preserve the maturing wines.

Sulphite as a sterilising agent

A solution of 15 g (½ oz) of sodium or potassium metabisulphite or 8 Campden tablets dissolved in 1 litre (2 pints) of warm water should be used for rinsing glassware and all other equipment before use. The solution can be kept in a tightly corked or screw-topped bottle for further use. A little may also be kept in demijohns that are not in use: if they are tightly corked they will remain bacteria-free until required. If containers are contaminated or dirty, they should first be thoroughly cleaned with a chlorine-based steriliser before being rinsed two or three times with cold water, then with the sulphite solution and finally with cold water again. It is a good policy to heat sterilise demijohns, airlocks, siphon tubes, etc. twice yearly. Small plastic items should not be heated above 65 °C (150 °F).

Strong sulphite solution for must and wine

Add 30 g (1 oz) of sodium metabisulphite to 284 ml (½ pint) cold water, bottle and cork. Use according to recipe instructions.

Pectin-destroying enzyme

This can be purchased in powder form. It helps to facilitate the pressing of fruit and increase the yield of juice, and will also prevent a haze in the finished wine. Most brands give the quantity required for each 4.5 litres (1 gal.), usually 5 g (1 tsp) per 2 kg (4½ lb) of fruit. In cold water extractions

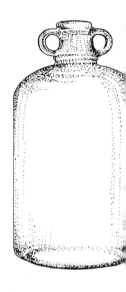

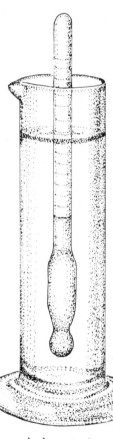

hydrometer in measuring jar

you can add it in the initial stages of preparation, but if the ingredients are heated, do not add until the liquid is at room temperature, because the heat destroys the enzymes.

Yeast nutrients

If the recipe does not include a high proportion of fruit or is made from flowers or vegetables, it will require nutrients for the development and growth of the yeast. Wines made with a high proportion of grapes or sultanas rarely need any additions. The main nutrients, ammonium phosphate, ammonium sulphate and magnesium sulphate, are usually sold under a proprietary brand name and contain all three chemicals.

Vitamin B_1 tablets

One tablet (3 mg) is usually sufficient for fruit and flower wines, but it is advisable to add two for wines made from vegetables or tinned fruits.

Acids and tannin

Most of the acids and tannin necessary will be obtained from the ingredients in the recipes, but a little extra will be required for flower and vegetable wines. Home winemaking stores sell packets of citric, malic or tartaric acids. The acidity may also be increased with lemon juice; 56 ml (2 fl oz) of lemon juice is equal to 7 g ($1/4$ oz) of tartaric acid. Commercially prepared tannin can also be purchased but it is generally only required in vegetable or some flower wines.

BASIC PRINPLES AND INGREDIENTS

METHODS OF WINEMAKING vary considerably from one person to another and the individual style of each winemaker is reflected in the finished product. If you have developed a successful formula, you should continue to use it, trying new experiments gradually and comparing the results. This chapter outlines the basic principles of winemaking; all the processes are described in greater detail in later chapters.

The recipes in this book are based on experiments I have made over the past thirty years. It was after I had spent a working holiday in the vineyards in the Rhinehessen that it became abundantly clear to me that the best wines are made only when all the essential ingredients have been extracted from the grapes. Quality wines are made from grapes with a high sugar content, with medium levels of tartaric and malic acids. In poor years an excessive amount of malic acid will still be discernible in the wine, even after several years of maturing, and although the sugar content will have been adjusted, it does not compare with the natural fruit sugars of the grapes. Bearing this in mind, I started compiling recipes with the object of obtaining as much natural sugar and acid as possible from the fruits selected to give a combination of acids, tannin and nutrients. As the grape is the perfect medium from which to get a vigorous and healthy fermentation plus good vinosity in the wine, the easiest and cheapest alternative must obviously be sultanas. They are of consistent quality with a very high sugar content, and their predominant acid is tartaric, which is essential to balance the malic and citric acids of our home-grown fruits. In recent years the availability of cartoned grape juice and grape concentrate have provided an alternative. In Germany and the Sauternes district of France the grapes that produce the sweet dessert wines are affected by the action of Botrytis cinerea, a fungus which attacks the grapes in warm humid conditions in late summer. This encourages a beneficial mould (*pourriture noble*) which extracts some of the liquid, leaving a sultana-type grape with a high concentration of sweet juice.

Most of the garden and country fruits used in winemaking have some natural sugars, but with high acid levels and pronounced flavours they need dilution with water in order to produce a drinkable wine within a reasonable maturing period. If sultanas or grape juice are used to provide as much natural sugar and tartaric acid as possible, the level of garden or hedgerow fruits should not exceed more than 1 to 1.5 kg ($2^{1/4}$–$3^{1/3}$ lb) per 4.5-litre demijohn (except in the case of apples and pears), otherwise the wine will contain an excessive amount of acid. As with grapes, the fruits will vary according to climatic conditions, and in very cold, wet summers it is advisable to reduce the garden fruits in proportion to the sultanas or grape juice used; conversely, in particularly hot summers the acids will be lower and the sugar content higher, so extra garden fruits may be added. Red wines will achieve more character by using red grape concentrate or red grape juice. As most grape concentrates are balanced and contain sufficient acid for a 4.5-litre demijohn, the quantity added to a country wine should not exceed more than 300 ml ($^{1/2}$ pint) per demijohn, except in making dessert wines.

In making sweet or dessert wines, which need more flavour, acid and body, the predominant fruits should be increased, with the addition of bananas, sultanas, grape concentrate or pears. As these wines are more prone to bacterial infection, the extra acid will help to protect them. It also plays an important part during the maturing period in combining with alcohol to form esters, which contribute so much to the bouquet and aroma. With residual sugar present the acid is essential to give interest and zest to the wine. During the process of fermentation the enzymes secreted by the yeast cells convert the sugars into ethyl alcohol and carbon dioxide. In order for the yeast to develop and multiply, the enzymes require an adequate amount of nutrients in the form of ammonium phosphate and ammonium sulphate. Grapes contain sufficient nutrients for the yeast, and recipes which combine a high proportion of grapes or sultanas with fresh fruits will rarely need any additions. Recipes based on dried, tinned or bottled fruits, however, benefit from the addition of 5 ml (1 tsp) of yeast nutrient plus a vitamin B_1 tablet. This applies also to flower and vegetable wines.

DIFFERENT METHODS OF FERMENTATION

In order to obtain as much natural sugar, acids, tannin and nutrients from the fruit as possible, many of the recipes given here recommend fermentation 'on the pulp' before the addition of sugar. This reduces the time necessary for fermentation, thus also reducing the risk of bacterial infection and the formation of other unwanted substances, which tend to get extracted by the alcohol as it is being produced. If no sugar has been added at this stage, the enzymes concentrate their activity on the extraction and conversion of the natural sugars in the fruit and also on the tannins, acids and nutrients. In a vigorous fermentation most fruit sugars will be extracted within three days, but an extra day or two may be necessary for red fruit wines when a deep red colour is required with plenty of tannin.

In order to obtain the maximum amount of alcohol from a pulp fermentation, it is essential to keep the container or bucket tightly covered once the fermentation is really established. As the fermentation gets going, the fruit pulp will be pushed to the top of the container by the force of the carbon dioxide gas, forming a cap. This must be broken up three or four times a day to facilitate a quicker extraction rate.

In this type of fermentation a hydrometer is of limited value (see page 6), so to estimate the amount of sugar present many books advise straining off enough liquid to test from the fruit pulp before fermentation takes place; this will give a rough guide to the extra sugar needed to obtain the desired alcoholic content. It does give a fairly accurate reading when you are using a grape concentrate, fresh grape juice, strained liquid after infusion in water or fruits with a low sugar content, but with fruits such as sultanas, raisins, dried apricots, figs and most of the pulpy fruits, the sugars are only completely extracted after two or three days of pulp fermentation. As a rough guide, one can estimate that just under half the weight of sultanas will be sugar.

The cold water extraction method is suitable for many soft fruits. A good extraction can be achieved if the fruit is washed, adding 10 ml (2 tsp) of sulphite solution to the water, drained and placed in the deep freezer, for 24 to 48 hours; this will allow the juice to flow more freely when thawed. Much harder fruits, i.e. apples, pears or gooseberries, can also be used, and this will make a lighter, fresher table wine than from a pulp fermentation. A hydrometer reading can be taken with this method, which will give a reasonably accurate indication of the sugar present. The extra sugar required may be added in the form of a syrup, or with grape concentrate, if used, once the fermentation has begun.

Deep red fruits can be pasteurised: in this method the fruit is heated to a temperature of 65 °C (150 °F), kept at this temperature for five minutes and then allowed to cool gradually. Boiling fruits to extract the juice used to be the common practice, but this has lost favour in the past few years, as it often imparts a 'cooked' flavour to the wine, which will lack the freshness of other methods.

Dried fruits such as apricots, peaches and prunes will make a cleaner wine if they are chopped and treated under the cold water system. It is essential, however, that root vegetables should be boiled and the liquid then strained off. If more than one or two bananas are used per gallon of wine, it is better to boil them for twenty minutes and strain off the liquid first, as otherwise the pulp tends to squeeze through the straining bag.

THE INGREDIENTS

It cannot be said that any one constituent of wine takes priority over another; they all have an essential part to play and the winemaker's art lies in balancing these constituents to their best advantage.

Fruits and flowers

In selecting ingredients always remember that the quality of your wines will depend on the quality of the ingredients. Fruits should be fully ripe and any mouldy ones must be discarded. Vegetables should be scrubbed thoroughly and flowers picked on a fine day and processed quickly. Frozen fruits can be used successfully for winemaking, as their cell walls collapse when thawed, making juice extraction easier. One of the advantages of freezing is that it helps to reduce costs, since fruit may be bought in the summer months when it is plentiful and kept to be augmented by other cheaper fruits in the autumn and winter.

Some country fruits may be difficult to obtain. Bilberries, for example, grow in profusion in some moorland areas but are almost unobtainable elsewhere. These can be purchased frozen, dried or bottled (the imported Polish ones are excellent), and a small quantity will impart a pleasant flavour to the wine. Sloes and bullaces may also be difficult to find, and if they are, you can substitute half damsons and half blackcurrants. Elderberries and blackberries are generally plentiful in the hedgerows, and fruits such as gooseberries, blackberries, redcurrants, cherries, raspberries, loganberries, damsons, plums, apples and pears very rarely fail in the garden, and can always be purchased quite readily in season. Fruits from warmer climates, such as apricots, peaches and grapes, are now available in the shops over quite a long period.

When choosing ingredients for home-made wines it is far better to use a blend of fruits rather than a single one. Some fruits naturally complement each other, while others do not harmonise. A bland fruit needs something to give interest and life to the wine. Apples and pears are good supplements to fruits such as apricots, peaches, pineapples and most of the red fruits. Strawberries on their own tend to produce a rather insipid wine with an overpowering bouquet, but adding a small quantity of blackcurrants will turn it into a very pleasant rosé. It is far better to blend fruits during the initial stages when they have a chance to harmonise rather than blending the wine at a later stage.

Flower wines receive much criticism, largely because the flowers' contribution is in the form of bouquet and aroma with very little vinosity. These wines should be light and early maturing. In order to balance the bouquet, some type of fruit which will not detract from the delicacy of the wine

11

should be used. The recipes for flower wines in this book are mainly based on the use of fruits that will contribute acidity and flavour but will not distract from the refinement created by the flowers. White sultanas, preferably the white Australian ones, or grape juice will provide extra natural sugar and give a vigorous fermentation.

Vegetable wines take a long time to mature, so many winemakers today cannot be bothered with them. Root vegetables need supplementing with fruit in order to give the wine character, acid and some natural sugars which the vegetables do not provide; nutrients must also be added to maintain a steady fermentation. Their contribution will be in body and flavour.

As already emphasised, the quality of the fruits used is of paramount importance in imparting their full flavour to the finished wine. They also provide a source for trace elements that are of such vital importance. A chemical analysis reveals that the average composition of wine is 85 per cent water, 14.5 percent acids, glycerol, alcohol, tannin and sugars, and the remaining 0.5 per cent the vital volatile and fixed constituents which transform it from the 'vin ordinaire' into the 'classic' class.

Acid

Acid is necessary to achieve a strong healthy fermentation, and it contributes greatly to the wine's flavour and character, as well as helping to protect the wine from bacterial infections and acting as an antioxidising agent. Without sufficient acid the wine would taste bland and medicinal.

The three main acids, tartaric, malic and citric, each play a different role, and the recipes given here are formulated to include fruits with some of each. The acid level or the pH of the must will influence the maturing period required for the wine. Quick maturing wines have a low acidity or a high pH reading; whereas wines which will be laid down for a few years need higher levels of acidity. Quality commercial white wines aim for an acid level of 8 g per litre as calculated in tartaric acid, or a pH reading of 3.2 to 3.3. Rosé wines are slightly less at 7 g per litre, and the initial reading for reds, before fermentation, about 7.5 g per litre. Red wine will undergo a pulp fermentation, which will extract colour, intensity and tannin. The astringency obtained from the tannin will help to protect it from bacterial damage and over-oxidation, but it will require a longer maturing period. Quick maturing red wines can be made from red fruit juices or by pasteurising the ingredients, but they will lack the intensity and character of a good red wine.

As winemakers become more experienced, they will be able to control the acidity of the wines to a greater degree of accuracy. Acid testing kits may be obtained from most home-brew shops, and these give detailed instructions on procedure. Most of the home testing wine kits are expressed as sulphuric acid, whereas in commercial winemaking tartaric acid is always used. As acids vary in strength, a wine giving a reading of 8 g per litre as expressed in tartaric acid would be 5.2 g as expressed in sulphuric acid. Likewise, 7 g per litre as tartaric would give a reading of 4.5 g sulphuric. A comparative acid table giving parts per thousand of various acids are given on page 148.

Tannin

Tannin is found significantly in the skins of fruits, with red fruits containing a higher proportion than white fruits. Fruits that have a high tannin concentration are elderberries, bilberries, sloes, damsons, grapes, including dried grapes (i.e. sultanas and raisins), pears and gooseberries.

One of the chief functions of tannin is to give astringency to the wine. This is particularly important for deep red wines, which rely on tannin to provide vigour and depth. It is also a major factor in conservation and clarification, as it combines with proteins and allied nitrogenous substances, which otherwise tend to give hazes in later stages. Because of their high tannin content, red wines taste very harsh when they are first made and take longer to mature.

Nutrients

Additional nutrients are sometimes necessary to 'feed' the yeast and maintain a vigorous fermentation. Most proprietary brands of yeast nutrient contain ammonium phosphate, ammonium sulphate and magnesium sulphate. Some contain only the former two ingredients, and if you live in a soft water area, a pinch of Epsom salts will replace the magnesium sulphate. One or two vitamin B_1 tablets are essential for vegetable and flower wines, but well-balanced fruit recipes with the right proportion of grapes or sultanas will ferment adequately with the nutrients extracted from the fruits.

Pectin

Most fruits contain pectin, which is essential in making jams and jellies; in winemaking it is not desirable, however, as it sometimes leaves an opaque haze in the wine. To overcome this problem pectin-destroying enzymes are used, which decompose the pectic substances in the early stages. Pectin-destroying enzymes are easily obtainable under a number of trade names, and a small quantity is recommended in the recipes given here.

Sugar

In making wine the main aim is to obtain all the sugars that are in the fruits, but however much attention is devoted to extracting as much natural sugar as possible from the ingredients, it will still be necessary to add sugar in order to obtain the required amount of alcohol. The cheapest and most suitable form to use is ordinary white granulated cane or beet sugar. This can be dissolved into the strained juice before adding to the demijohn, but with dessert wines, which need continual additions as the SG drops, it will be added as sugar syrup.

Yeast

No wine can be produced without the aid of yeasts. Their purpose is to break down organic substances by means of the enzymes they secrete; in winemaking it is necessary for the sugars to be broken down into alcohol and carbon dioxide.

There are many types of yeasts, some beneficial in winemaking and others termed 'wild'. Yeasts exist on all fruits and can be seen on the skins of some (known as the bloom).

Both good and wild yeasts will reach the fermentation jars when you are making wine. The wild yeasts will multiply if they have access to oxygen, but if a small amount of sulphite is added to the prepared fruit, the sulphur dioxide released will displace the oxygen, so inhibiting their growth. The wine yeasts can more easily withstand sulphite, and as they are anaerobic (that is, they can develop without oxygen) they will soon build up an active colony and rapidly gain control. Furthermore, they are protected by the build-up of carbon dioxide and increasing alcohol content, which the wild yeasts are unable to tolerate. For this reason it is essential not to expose the fruit pulp for any length of time once fermentation has begun.

Various wine yeasts are in plentiful supply in most winemaking shops. Do not use brewer's or baker's yeasts, as these may impart a yeasty flavour to the wine and they generally have a poorer alcohol tolerance. Wine yeasts are available in cultured or dried form. The cultured yeasts are expensive but are more true to type and worth while if you intend to make several batches. The next most desirable are in sealed tablet form. They can also be purchased in tubs or jars, but the risk of infection is then greater, although many winemakers appear to use them without any problems. It is advisable to use a type of yeast as near as possible to the character of wine you intend to make: Burgundy or Bordeaux for table reds, Hock or Chablis for the light whites, Sauternes for sweeter whites, and Tokay for dessert reds.

Yeasts require an acidic solution with nutrients and vitamins in order to multiply and create an active fermentation. In wines containing a high proportion of fresh fruits these elements will be extracted by pulp fermentation; but if fruits are infused in water or pasteurised before pressing, some extra nutrient may be necessary. If only a small quantity of fruit is used or the main ingredients are vegetables or flowers, these essential additives must be included to ensure a healthy fermentation.

Yeasts are inhibited if too high a ratio of sugar to water is added before a vigorous colony has been formed. This is a trap that many beginners fall into: too much sugar syrup is added initially to the strained must, resulting in an over-concentrated solution which kills off the yeast. What happens, in simple terms, is that water in the fermenting yeast cells is transferred through the yeast cell walls to dilute the highly concentrated sugar solution; if this process of osmosis is too extreme, the cells – which are 50 per cent water – become dehydrated and eventually die.

Glycerine
Glycerine is a product of fermentation, and the quantity present in wine is quite high, sweet wines usually having twice the amount of the drier types. It creates a softness and roundness which is of great importance in the finished wines.

Water
Country wines rely on water, and several litres are included in many recipes. If you have a clean water supply, there is no need to boil the water before use, but if in doubt or if it contains a taint of chlorine, boil it first or use bottled water.

Sulphite

The burning of sulphur candles or cloth wicks in empty casks to produce a sterilising gas was the normal practice in all wine-producing countries when casks were the only vessels for storing wines. The burning sulphur combined with oxygen to form sulphur dioxide, which killed or inhibited spoilage organisms. Today winemakers are able to buy crystals of sodium or potassium metabisulphite, either loose or in tablet form, which are marketed under the name of Campden tablets. They should be renewed yearly in order for them to be effective when added to must or wine, using the older ones for making the sterilising solution. Sulphite plays an important part in the winemaking process. It is added to the freshly crushed fruit or must, inhibiting and destroying unwanted mould and bacteria. It is important not to exceed the recommended dose in the preparation of the fruits, as this will slow down the onset of fermentation. When fermentation is completed a heavy deposit of debris and dead yeast cells settles at the bottom of the jar. After 48 hours, siphon the wine again and add 2 crushed Campden tablets; this is equivalent to 100 parts per million (p.p.m.) of sulphite, which will serve as an antioxidant and control undesirable micro-organisms. As it combines with acetaldehydes and other binding compounds present in the wine, so the quantity of free sulphur dioxide will be reduced, and when the wine is racked or siphoned again, a light sulphiting at the rate of 50 p.p.m. or 1 Campden tablet should be used.

In making sweet wines, which contain a higher quantity of fruit, much of the sulphite is used up in combining with sugars and acids to form bisulphite compounds, so the amount of sulphur dioxide left to protect wine against bacterial infection will be greatly reduced. It is critical that these fuller, sweeter wines will need extra sulphite when fermentation is complete.

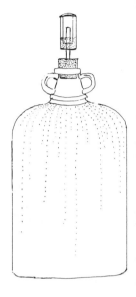

Reaction of yeast in demijohn

Sorbate

Sorbic Acid, which is used in food preservation, is found naturally in rowan tree berries and in unripe sorb apples. It is sold commercially in the form of white crystals and is widely used to control yeast growth in sweet wines.

The high degree of alcohol in dessert wines will help inhibit a secondary fermentation, but if a low alcohol table wine is left with a high degree of sugar and low acidity, it is vulnerable. It is then advisable to add sorbic acid in conjunction with sulphite to prevent any action of the lactic acid bacteria (lactobacilli) from producing a geranium-like smell, spoiling the bouquet of the wine.

The quantity of sorbic acid needed will depend on the alcoholic content and acidity of the wine.

Wines with a pH of 3.4 or above, with an alcoholic content of 11 per cent, will need 125 mg per litre of sorbic acid and $1/2$ crushed Campden tablet (25 mg per litre of sulphite) dissolved in a little water before adding. The quantity for a demijohn of 4.5 litres would be 562 mg sorbic acid and 112 mg sulphite (2 crushed Campden tablets).

Wines with a pH of 3.2 to 3.3 will require 75 mg to 100 mg of sorbic acid plus 25 mg per litre of sulphite, i.e. 340 mg to 450 mg sorbic acid and 112 mg sulphite per demijohn.

PREPARATION OF THE MUST AND CONTROL OF FERMENTATION

THE DICTIONARY DEFINITION of must is 'unfermented or only partially fermented juice'. It is only when the fermentation is complete that the must becomes wine.

The must is a combination of ingredients from which the wine will be made, and its quality and character will depend to a large extent on the choice and preparation of ingredients at this critical stage. The way the ingredients are processed will enhance or damage the final quality of the wine: the ripeness and condition of the fruits or the amount of sunshine on the flowers are important factors.

Provided that the ingredients are in good condition, the method of preparation and control of fermentation play the next most important parts. The choice of preparation falls into four categories:

1. *pulp fermentation*: the extraction of sugar, acids, nutrients, etc. by the yeast enzymes
2. *cold water infusion*: steeping the ingredients in water before adding the yeasts
3. *pasteurisation*: extraction by heat
4. *juice extraction*: by force or pressure

All will give satisfactory results, but the finished wines will have different characteristics according to the method used. These are described in detail on pages 17–24.

16

THE RIGHT TEMPERATURE

The control of temperature also plays a crucial part in the retention of bouquet and flavour. In fermenting small quantities of wine it is essential to keep the jars at temperatures of 16 °C (60 °F) for white wines, although strains of yeast have been developed which will ferment at temperatures as low as 10 °C (50 °F). Red wines need a slightly higher temperature of 18 °C (65 °F). During the vigorous primary fermentation these lower temperatures are adequate, but as it nears completion the fermentation will slow down and may be moved to a warmer place. When larger quantities are fermented heat is retained within the bulk of the wine and so fermentation will take place satisfactorily in cooler surroundings. (In Germany and California it is common practice to ferment commercially at low temperatures with the result that the wine produced retains more bouquet and flavour.)

ACTIVATING THE YEAST

Many wine yeasts will activate by adding them directly to the bulk, but as it is important for the fermentation to start quickly, to alleviate the risk of bacterial problems, it is advisable to activate the specialised tablet yeasts or yeast cultures 24 hours in advance so that a sizeable colony is established before adding to the bulk. A suitable starter medium can be prepared as follows

Yeast starter
Dissolve 1 dessertspoon sugar in 142 ml (¹/₄ pint) warm water, add the juice from ¹/₂ lemon (approx. 25 ml) and a small pinch of yeast nutrient and one yeast tablet or 5 ml teaspoon of yeast culture. Pour into a sterilised bottle; the solution should three-quarters fill the bottle. Plug the top with cotton wool and stand in a warm place (21 °C, 70 °F) for 24 hours.

When adding the active yeast starter to the must it is a good idea to leave a small amount in the bottom of the bottle and top it up with a little more starter medium in case the development of the colony is retarded by the level of sulphite still remaining in the must. If this happens, the remaining yeast starter can be added in 24 hours, or if not needed, it can be used for the next batch. It should be stored in the refrigerator, but do not keep it for longer than a week, as the risk of bacterial infection is always present.

METHODS OF EXTRACTION
1 Pulp fermentation

All equipment must be thoroughly cleaned. It should be rinsed with a sulphite solution and then rinsed again with cold water. All fruits must be free from moulds. Hard fruits can be washed, sultanas should be washed and chopped or lightly liquidised, and soft fruits crushed. When making flower wines petals should be carefully checked for foreign bodies and all the green calyx should be removed or it will impart a bitter flavour. Remove as many stones as possible from apricots, plums, cherries, bullaces, sloes, etc. (care should be taken not to crack the stones, as this, too, will give an unpleasant flavour).

Starter bottle plugged with cotton wool

17

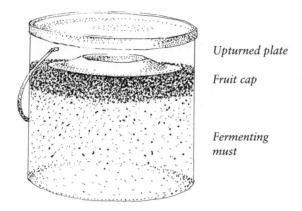

Upturned plate

Fruit cap

Fermenting must

Add the recommended quantity of cold water, pectin-destroying enzyme, sulphite solution or Campden tablets, yeast nutrient and vitamin B1 tablets. Stir well and cover. Leave for 24 hours before adding the active yeast starter, which should be carefully poured into the top of the must. Do not stir into the bulk at this stage, but wait for about 12 hours until an active colony has developed before stirring it in. In order to extract the maximum sugar and acid from the fruits it is essential to keep the fruit cap submerged as far as possible. The cap should be broken up several times each day, and this can be done most easily with an upturned plate kept on top of the must.

The bucket must always be kept tightly covered. If the cover does not fit well, place a sheet of polythene sheeting over the top and secure with a strong elastic band before putting on the cover. This will also be effective in the case of larger bins.

If the fermentation is really active, two days is usually adequate to extract all the sugars and acids from the pulp, but a red wine may require an extra day or two to get a deep red colour and extra tannin for its development. After the pulp has fermented for the period recommended in the recipe, place the sterile straining bag into another container of similar size and pour in the fermenting must. Lift the edges of the bag and agitate it slowly from side to side so that most of the liquid drains through. Pour this into the 4.5-litre demijohn and fit an airlock. Twist the top of the straining bag lightly, and after washing the original bucket free of any remaining fruit pulp, place the 'pudding' of the pulp on an upturned glass dish in the bucket. Replace the lid immediately and leave for 12 hours, when the remaining must will have drained free. (If you are making a large quantity in a bin, use an upturned plastic bucket to support the straining bag.) This method helps to reduce the risk of bacterial infection as the fermenting pulp and must still continue to build up carbon dioxide, thus protecting the wine during the straining period.

Pour the remaining strained must into the fermenting jar and add the sugar syrup (see overleaf). The jar should be only seven-eighths full to allow for any excessive frothing which may occur. After a few days, top up to the neck of the jar with cold boiled water.

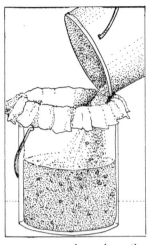

*pour must through sterile
straining bag*

twist the top of the bag

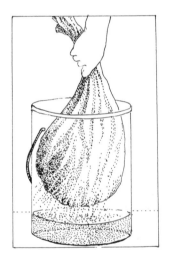

*lift bag to allow must
to drain*

*place bag on upturned bowl
to drain further*

Sugar solution or sugar syrup
*Dissolve approximately 500 g of sugar to 300 ml of water (1lb to
¹/₂ pint) over a slow heat. Extra quantities should be made in the
same proportions.*

strained must   *seven-eigths full after*   *airlock filled*   *topped up after*
addition of sugar   *a few days*

2 Cold water infusion

This method particularly applies to the making of white wines in order to
achieve a delicate, refreshing and clean wine. The fruits enhanced by cold
water infusion are apples, apricots, gooseberries and pears. The fruit should
be washed with 10ml (2 tsp) of sulphite solution in water to get rid of any
debris, which will float to the top and can be removed. Drain the fruit and
place the required amount in a plastic bag and put in the freezer. As the
fruit freezes, ice crystals will form within the fruit, which, when thawed,
will allow the juice to flow more freely. After the fruit is frozen, remove and
place in a plastic bucket and pour boiling water over the fruit, ensuring the
water covers the fruit. It should be stirred, and when it reaches room temperature the berries or apples will be soft enough to be easily crushed by
hand. At this stage stir in the pectin-destroying enzyme, nutrients, vitamin
B1 tablet and 5ml (1 tsp) of strong sulphite solution, or 1 crushed Campden
tablet. Leave for 24 hours before straining through a double nylon bag,
pressing gently on the nylon bag to extract as much juice as possible.

> **Strong sulphite solution for must and wine**
> *Add 30 g (1 oz) of sodium or potassium metabisulphite to 284 ml*
> *(½ pint) of water. Store in a screw-topped bottle.*

The extracted juice should be left for 24 hours so that any traces of pulp
can settle; then siphon off the clear juice into a demijohn. It is important
not to take any pulp solids, as these will give an undesirable coarseness to
an otherwise delicate wine. Once the juice has been extracted it will be necessary to calculate the quantity of sugar required to increase the SG to a
level of 1.080 and this will give an alcoholic content of 10.5% in the finished wine. This is the optimum level to balance this delicate wine but the
alcoholic level can be increased for strong flavoured or for red wines.

Most garden fruits, except grapes, do not contain more than 6% to 10% sugar. When 1.5 kg (3⅓ lb) of fruit is processed in water an approximate SG reading of 1.020 to 1.030 per demijohn should be obtained; this will, of course, depend on the sweetness of the fruit. As 750 g (1 lb 10 oz) of sugar will give a rise of 0.062 this, together with the fruit of approximately 1.020, gives a total SG of 1.082 (see SG table on page 147).

When this has been dissolved and added to the demijohn it should be topped up with water to seven-eighths; this will leave an air space for the primary fermentation to take place and allow space for a final sugar adjustment to be made. A hydrometer reading should now be taken to assess if extra sugar is needed.

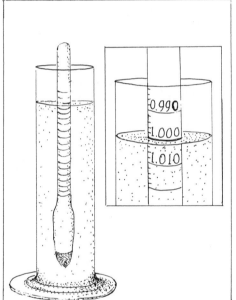

hydrometer in water   strained must

Note: The hydrometer indicates the density or specific gravity of a liquid being measured compared with the density of water. In a heavy, syrupy solution the hydrometer will float high, giving a high reading, whereas in water or after fermentation is completed, it will float just off the bottom of the measuring jar, giving a low reading. The temperature will influence the hydrometer reading and it is advisable for the liquid to be 15 °C (60 °F) to get an accurate reading.

When an SG reading has been recorded, add the yeast from the starter bottle and fit an airlock. Keep the jar in a temperature of about 18 °C (65 °F). After the first vigorous fermentation has subsided, the jar may be topped up with a weak sugar syrup. If the must reading at the beginning of the fermentation was 1.074, an increase of 0.006 is required, so the quantity needed will be 72 g of sugar (see page 147 for specific gravity calculations).

As the fermentation nears completion, the specific gravity will drop to between 0.990 and 1.000. If a dry wine is required, the SG reading should be at the lower figure. However, many winemakers like there to be some residual sugar; this can be achieved by sweetening the wine to an SG of 0.996 before bottling, when all the yeast cells have been eliminated. The wine should then be removed to a cool place.

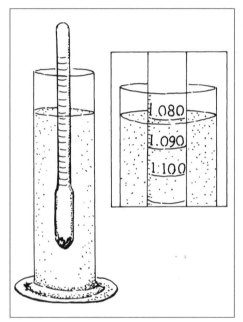

after adding sugar

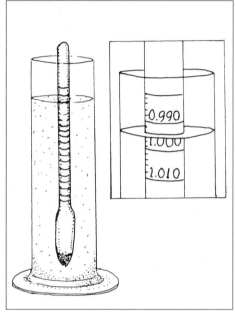

fermentation completed

3 Pasteurisation

A good extraction rate can be achieved when making red wines by heating or pasteurising the ingredients for a controlled period. This will extract more colour and flavour without including a high proportion of acids and tannin, which is inevitable with some red fruits if fermented on the pulp. The wine will be lighter in texture and will mature more quickly, but it will lack some of the character of the deep red wines. Fruits particularly suitable for this method are elderberries, sloes, bullaces, blackcurrants, damsons, bilberries and blackberries.

Pasteurisation prevents bacterial spoilage and eliminates the necessity to add sulphite to the must in the preparation state. As the ingredients are not boiled, the wine retains a clean, fresh flavour which is destroyed with boiling.

The ingredients should be washed and chopped. Add the required amount of cold water and heat to 65 °C (150 °F), maintaining this temperature for five minutes. Remove from the heat and leave to cool. If you do not have a culinary thermometer, bring the required amount to the boil, add all the ingredients, remove from the heat and stir for a few minutes. When cool pour into a covered bucket, adding the pectin-destroying enzyme, vitamin B1 tablet and yeast nutrient. Leave for 24 hours, then strain and take the hydrometer reading to assess the sugar present in the must. Calculate the amount of sugar necessary to bring the SG up to 1.080 (see page 147) but do not add the sugar at this stage. Pour into a demijohn with the yeast starter and plug the jar with cotton wool. The fermentation should be active within 24 hours when sugar may be added.

4 Juice Extraction

Centrifugal juice extractors have a limited use and are suitable for some fruits, for example apples, oranges, raspberries, loganberries and blackberries. Most fruits are strongly flavoured and have a high acid content, so they will need to be diluted with water.

After you have measured the SG and calculated the amount of sugar needed, pour the liquid into a demijohn with the pectin-destroying enzyme, nutrients and yeast starter. Once the fermentation is active the sugar may be added. If you have a really large quantity of grapes to process, it may be

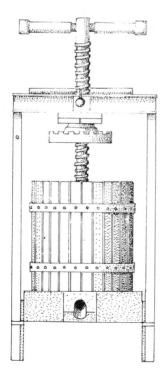

necessary to buy a fruit press. These can sometimes be hired from the Home-made Wine and Beer shops. If the grapes are fully ripe, they can be crushed by hand or placed in a bucket and crushed with a sterilised wooden block. Leave the crushed grapes in a covered bin or bucket overnight with 1 crushed Campden tablet or 5 ml (1 tsp) of strong sulphite solution and 10 ml (2 tsp) of pectin-destroying enzyme for 7 kg (15 lb) of grapes. This will facilitate the pressing and give a better yield of juice.

Whatever the extraction method chosen, as soon as the must is poured into the fermentation jars it will follow a similar pattern. During the first few days fermentation will be very vigorous, and this will be apparent from the speed of the popping airlock releasing the carbon dioxide. After several days the rhythm becomes slower as the available sugar decreases, and fermentation will finally cease. In table wines this process should be completed in two to three weeks, when the SG should have dropped to below 1.000

Social and dessert wines need to have a higher alcoholic content, which is achieved by adding more sugar syrup. In making these wines, sugar syrup must be added as soon as the hydrometer reading drops to a SG of 1.005, bringing it up to 1.015 again. For social wines this process should be repeated once more. In order to achieve the higher alcoholic content for dessert wines, additions of sugar syrup should be added each time the SG drops to 1.005 until fermentation finally ceases. Up to six or seven additions may be necessary before the level of alcohol finally kills the yeasts. As a rough guide, the SG of social wines should be in the region of 1.005 to 1.010, and the fruit full-bodied dessert wines from 1.015 to 1.030.

When the fermentation has finished, remove the jar to a cool place and rack according to the instructions in the following chapter.

RACKING, CLEARING, BOTTLING AND MATURING

RACKING

THE HEAVY DEPOSIT, known as lees, which forms on the bottom of the jar as fermentation proceeds is mainly composed of yeast debris and insoluble salts. If these dead yeast cells and debris are left for too long, they begin to decompose, with the consequent production of 'off' flavours. It is of paramount importance, therefore, as soon as fermentation is completed, to siphon off the clearing wine from the lees (see illustration page 26). Top up to the neck of the jar with a little cold water; this is essential to prevent oxidation. Replace the airlock and remove to a cooler place. After two days siphon again into a clean jar, adding 2 crushed Campden tablets or 10 ml (2 tsp) of strong sulphite solution. Top up again with cold water, but this time replace the airlock with a cork bung. This quantity of sulphite will inhibit most remaining yeast cells and give a high protection against bacterial problems.

The wine will need racking again after three weeks, with the addition of another crushed Campden tablet or 5 ml (1 tsp) of strong sulphite solution.

It is important not to aerate the wine too much during the racking process, as this will reduce the proportion of sulphur dioxide remaining in the wine. The siphon tube should be placed at the bottom of the receiving vessel to prevent aeration.

Place the jar on a table or draining board carefully so as not to disturb the sediment. Put an empty sterile jar below on the floor. Take the siphon tube, which should be about 2 metres (6 feet) long, and place the tube in the jar above the sediment, taking care not to disturb it. Suck the wine gently up the tube, and when it is full quickly put your index finger over the end of the tube and lower it into the bottom of the receiving jar. The wine will flow freely as long as the end of the tube in the upper jar is submerged. As the upper jar empties gently tilt it to remove as much liquid as possible without disturbing the sediment. Top up with cold water and replace the bung.

CLEARING

The wine should be stored in a cool dark place to mature. This is not always possible in modern houses, but try to select a place where the temperature does not vary too greatly. It is better to store it in a constant temperature of 16 °C (60 °F) than in one which changes rapidly with weather

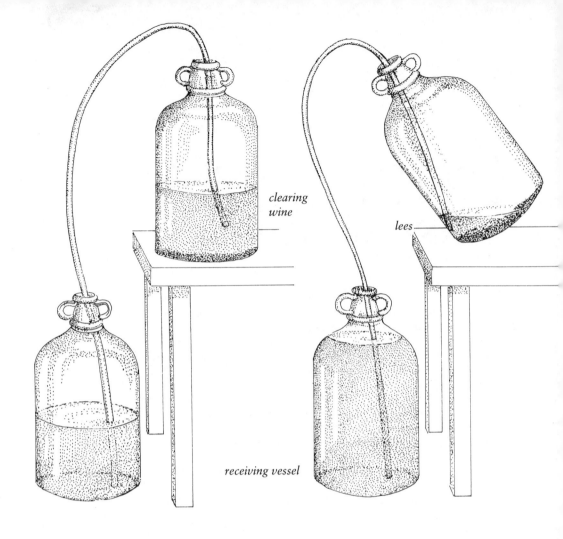

clearing wine

lees

receiving vessel

conditions. Some wines will clear quite quickly but others need a longer maturing period. As soon as a deposit forms which covers the bottom of the jar, you should rack again. It is very important at this stage to avoid oxidising the wine, so make certain that the siphon tube is always kept at the bottom of the receiving vessel.

The recipes recommend a large dose of sulphite after the second racking and a smaller dose on the third racking in order to prevent bacterial or secondary fermentation that will cause a haze. Except for an infected wine, these are the only doses the wine should receive. Most red wines will clear fairly quickly on account of their high tannin content. The negative charged tannins are attracted to the positively charged proteins in suspension to form insoluble groups, which by their weight precipitate or settle to the bottom. White wines, which also have proteins in suspension, especially if they are fermented on the pulp, do not, however, contain so much tannin. It is necessary to remove these minute particles in the wine by using a negatively charged fining. The most satisfactory method is by using a form of Wyoming clay called bentonite. It is used by commercial winemakers as it has the special ability to combine with protein particles, which will then fall out of suspension. It is not easy to mix owing to its powdery consistency.

The amount required should be placed in a small bottle with 25 cl of water and shaken several times during the day when it will eventually form a glutinous liquid which can be added to be bulk.

Bentonite for a 4.5-litre Demijohn
Put 25 cl of water in a small bottle and add 4 g of bentonite. Shake well and leave for an hour before shaking again. Repeat until the bentonite has formed a glutinous liquid.

The quantity of bentonite needed will vary, as some wines require more than others to achieve star brightness, but if too much is used, a negative haze will be caused by this excess. During our commercial winemaking it was usually found necessary to add 0.75 grams to 1 gram of bentonite per litre of wine. Our records over 15 years show that generally 1 gram per litre (equal to 4.5 g per 4.5-litre demijohn) was sufficient for most wines.

Technical improvements are continually being made and the trade has produced some simple and effective wine clearing kits. These are based on the addition of 5 ml (1 tsp) of Kieselsol and 5 ml (1 tsp) of gelatine to each 4.5-litre demijohn. These are available from the Home-made Wine and Beer Shops and full instructions are included in the kits.

FILTERING

To obtain a 'star bright' quality it will be necessary to filter the wine using cellulose filters. Inexpensive filter kits can be bought for small quantities of wine, or if you are making several gallons, you can use the large hand pump filters. Both are very effective and often can be hired from Home-made Wine and Beer Shops. To prevent a filter taint you should flush the filter through with water for 15 minutes, followed by a small quantity of wine which should then be discarded.

Filtering gives a final polish to the wine, but do not attempt to remove a heavy sediment or haze in this way, for it will just clog the filter.

BOTTLING

Throughout the making of the wine great care has been taken to ensure that it is free from microbial organisms. It is important during the final stage that every effort is made to maintain this standard so that the wine will keep and improve in bottle; carelessness or indifference at this time could ruin the efforts that have gone into the earlier stages. If careful racking has been carried out, dry red and white table wines should have adequate free sulphur dioxide remaining in them to give protection during their bottled life, but if the wines are going to be sweetened, extra protection will be necessary against bacterial and secondary fermentation. Many winemakers prefer to take the edge off the dryness by adding 30 g (1 oz) of sugar to 4.5 litres (1 gal.) of wine at this stage; if more than this quantity is used, it is advisable to add 2 crushed Campden tablets or 10 ml (2 tsp) of strong sulphite solution before bottling, plus sorbic acid (see page 15).

When selecting bottles make sure they are in keeping with the type of wine produced. A deep red wine is traditionally bottled in a green Bordeaux

or Burgundy type bottle. Not only does this add to the anticipation as the wine is poured, but the quality of the wine is maintained, for strong light will adversely affect both the colour and the quality of red wines. White or rosé wines can be bottled in Hock bottles, or, if they are kept in a dark place, in white Bordeaux or tinted Burgundy bottles.

If the bottles you are using are not new, they should be thoroughly cleaned with a chlorine steriliser and then rinsed two or three times in cold water. Rinse them finally with a mild sulphite solution (1 Campden tablet to 1.1 litres/2 pints of water) and drain in a sterile bucket for 20 minutes before use. New bottles should be rinsed with sulphite solution and drained in the same way.

Care should be taken to obtain good quality corks, which must be smooth and even-grained. Before bottling, soak them for two hours in a mild sulphite solution; do not use boiling water or the corks will lose some of their elasticity and become hard. As the corks will tend to float to the surface, a weighted container should be placed over them to keep them submerged.

The wine may now be siphoned from the jar into the clean bottles, following the same procedure as racking by placing the bottles at a lower level so that the wine flows freely. When the bottle is nearly full place your index finger over the end of the tube and transfer it to another bottle. Bottles should be filled to within about 6cm (2^1/2in.) of the top, allowing an air space of 2cm (^{3}/4in.) between the wine and the cork.

A hand corking tool may be used to drive the cork home flush with the top of the bottle, and a plastic or foil capsule can then be fitted over the cork. The wine should be clearly labelled with details of the variety, type and date of production; attractive labels can be found in winemaking shops and will add to the appearance of your wine. Alternatively, winemakers may relish the challenge of producing their own unique labels at home on their desktop computers either by creating decorative flower borders or imposing a background picture of their house and so establishing their own trademark!

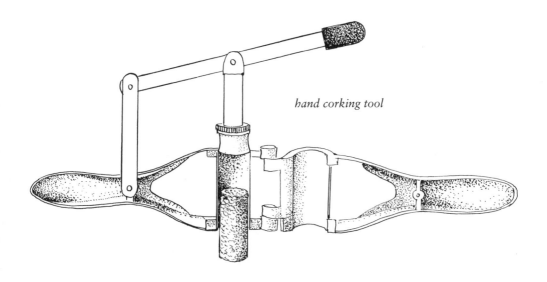

hand corking tool

MATURING WINE

A note at the end of each recipe advises that the wine should be allowed to mature in bulk for a given period. This is an important step and may need some clarification.

There are two stages of maturation, the first occurs when the wine is stored in bulk. The oxygen content will be high as it has been continually subjected to a series of processing operations, e.g. racking, stabilising, etc. Although a limited amount of oxygen in the wine is essential for its development, too much oxygen absorbed into the wine, perhaps by excessive exposure to air during racking, can be a fault affecting taste and bouquet.

The second stage occurs by a chemical reaction when the wine is bottled. This ageing is part of a complex process involving the reduction of malic acid, succinic acid and other components in the absence of air, and this has a direct effect on the formation of the bouquet and taste of the wine.

When stored in a cool temperature, the wine gradually mellows, losing its early harshness. The fruity fragrance of a new wine is replaced by a delicate complexity and fine bouquet. The tannins in red wine will, in the course of time, precipitate out in the form of crystals and give a softer and more mellow taste.

Bottles should be stored on their sides so that the corks do not dry out and allow unnecessary oxidisation.

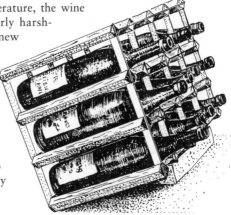

put crate nearly level or corks will dry out

29

$\mathcal{S}$OME POTENTIAL PROBLEMS

IF THE BASIC RULES of winemaking are followed with reasonable care, few difficulties should arise, but occasionally failures will occur. Some may be capable of remedy, others not; but knowing the reasons may prevent you making the same mistakes again. It is important to keep detailed records of the ingredients used and the method of juice extraction and fermentation so that as wines reach maturity you can assess and compare their merits and defects.

Stuck fermentation
One of the most common faults, especially among beginners, is a 'stuck' fermentation. This means that fermentation has ceased before all the sugar has been fermented by the yeasts, leaving an excessively sweet wine. There are several different causes of a stuck fermentation, and it is best to check first for faults that are the easiest to remedy.

1. Temperature
This should be in the region of 16–20 °C (60–65 °F). If the temperature has dropped to 10 °C (50 °F) or less, there is a possibility that the yeast cells have become dormant, so the must should be moved to a warmer place when they will gradually become more active. If, on the other hand, the wine has been kept in a temperature of 27–29 °C (80–85 °F) this heat will have killed the yeast cells and the must will have to be restarted (see 5, below).

2. Nutrients
Check that you added nutrients and vitamin B_1. If the must has a low fruit content or vegetable and flower wines are being made, it is essential to add 5g (1 tsp) of nutrients and 1 vitamin B_1 tablet.

3. Acid
Yeasts ferment more actively in an acid medium, so check whether the must lacks acid. If it tastes insipid, add 5 g (1 tsp) tartaric acid or 56 ml (2 fl oz) of lemon juice.

4. Yeasts
It is important to use the correct yeast for the type of wine intended to be made, as some yeasts have a higher alcoholic tolerance than others. When making sweet or dessert wines especially, always use a yeast suitable for the purpose. As already noted, it is best to use yeasts in tablet or cultured form, since with drums there is a risk of deterioration if they are exposed to the air or kept too long in storage.

WINE RECORD SHEET

TYPE **Goosebury 3. Page 69** DATE **10.2.01**

INGREDIENTS **1.5 kg gooseberies, 1 kg pears, 1 litre white grape juice, 1 tsp pectic enzyme, 1 tsp yeast nutrient, vitamin B1 tablet, Chablis type yeast, 2 litres water**

TYPE OF FERMENTATION **Cold water infusion**

DATE STRAINED **13.2.01**   SG READING **1.015**

ADDITIVES **1 litre grape juice. 700 g sugar**

SG READING **1.082**

DATE **20.2.01**   FININGS USED **4 g Bentonite**

FERMENTATION COMPLETED **28.2.01** SG READING **0.992**

1st RACKING **28.2.01** TREATMENT **Remove to cool place**

2nd RACKING **3.3.01** ADDITIVES **2 crushed Campden tablets**

3rd RACKING **15.3.01** ADDITIVES **1 crushed Campden tablet**

COMMENTS **Wine clearing, heavy deposit**

4th RACKING **15.4.01**

COMMENTS **Very clear with good bouquet, rather harsh.**

DATE OF BOTTLING **30.8.01** SG READING **0.992**

COMMENTS **Ready to bottle, but very dry, needs sweetening to raise SG from 0.992 to 0.998**

ADDITIVES **Dissolve 66 g sugar in a little wine plus 1 crushed Campden tablet**

NOTES **If a slightly sweeter wine is preferred, raise SG to 1.004 by adding 130 g sugar plus 560 mg sorbic acid (a small level teaspoon) and 2 crushed Campden tablets**

5. Sugar

As the yeast cells are inhibited by sugar in solution, it is necessary to build up a strong colony of yeast cells before adding too much sugar. If the mistake has already been made, however, the only satisfactory remedy is to restart the fermentation.

Make a starter bottle (see page 17), then check the quantity of sugar added to the 'stuck' must. If this was more than 1.1 kg (2½ lb) plus a total of 1.4 kg (3 lb) of fruit, the quantity was above the alcoholic tolerance of the yeast and will need diluting with water. Take 568 ml (1 pint) of the must and 568 ml (1 pint) of cold water and pour into another demijohn with an active yeast starter; plug with cotton wool. When the fermentation is active add another 568 ml (1 pint) of must but only 284 ml (½ pint) of water; when active again, gradually add the remaining must and fit an airlock.

As dilution with water will have increased the volume of must to more than 4.5 litres (1 gal.), the fermenting surplus can be placed in a bottle with a neck wide enough to take a bung and airlock; a milk bottle (the old type) or soft drinks bottle is ideal. This can be used for topping up at a later stage.

Yeast haze

In the normal way as the wine completes its fermentation, the thick haze caused by the yeast cells will gradually sink to the bottom of the jar, building up a heavy deposit. If the specific gravity has dropped to 0.990 or below, rack the wine, leave for two days and rack again, adding the recommended amount of Campden tablets or sodium or potassium metabisulphite. This should eliminate any remaining yeasts.

Pectin haze

Hazes caused by pectin can be prevented in the preparation stage by adding a pectin-destroying enzyme (see page 18). If in doubt, a simple test can be carried out to establish whether pectin is present. Take 15 ml (1 tbsp) of wine, place it in a small bottle or glass and add three times the amount of methylated spirit, giving the bottle or glass a quick swirl. If a gelatinous clot forms, pectin is present. This may be remedied at this stage by adding one of the pectin-destroying enzymes, preferably a liquid one, using the amount recommended on the manufacturer's instructions. Leave for a few days to allow to settle before racking again.

Protein haze

Many wines made with a large proportion of fruit often show a fine haze caused by protein instability. In red wine the high tannin content helps precipitation by coagulating proteins that are in suspension. White wines are often more difficult to clear, however, and fruity type wines need a longer period in bulk to mature (see pages 25–27 on Clearing).

Tartrates

This deposit occurs during the maturing period of red and white wines. The crystals form a deposit at the bottom of the jar, and in red wines they are encrusted with particles of colouring material. Their precipitation can be hastened by placing the demijohn in the refrigerator at a very low temperature

(1 °C, 34 °F). The wine should be held there for a few days until the perceptible tartrates have crystallised out. Then rack the wine into a clean demijohn or bottles. The wine is rarely cloudy as a result of this process.

Enzymatic oxidation

Wines made from over-ripe fruit may be affected by an enzyme which accelerates the oxidation of tannins, causing a chocolate brown haze followed by a yellowish-brown deposit in red wines, and a deep golden haze with a slight deposit in whites. In both cases the wine will taste and smell 'maderised', i.e. like caramel or burnt sugar. Once the wines have changed their character in this way there is no cure. Preventive measures are essential: the correct use of sulphite, care in racking, and maintaining jars to full capacity after fermentation ceases.

Hydrogen sulphide

Unlike micro-organisms that grow in the presence of air, hydrogen sulphide develops in the absence of free oxygen, hence the term 'anaerobic'. It has a disagreeable smell of rotten eggs. Purchased fruit which has received a sulphur spray prior to harvesting will allow some strains of yeast to reduce the elemental sulphur on the fruits into hydrogen sulphide. It is therefore advisable to wash and drain them before use. Sulphite used to terminate a fermentation can also cause a problem. If you wish to stop a fermentation before the wine becomes too dry, place the demijohn in a cool place and after 24 hours rack the wine into a clean jar. Leave for another two days in a cool temperature to reduce the colony of active yeast cells before racking again and adding the sulphite (2 Campden tablets or 10 ml/2 tsp of strong sulphite solution).

If a problem with hydrogen sulphide does occur it can be helped by adding 2 crushed Campden tablets or 10 ml (2 tsp) strong sulphite solution, but wines affected with this problem will lose much of their character.

Malo-lactic fermentation

In wines with a high malic acid content a secondary fermentation may occur if sulphite levels are too low. This is due to the action of lactobacilli breaking down the malic acid to form lactic acid and carbon dioxide. Some winemakers like to encourage this, as the lactic acid will produce a softer wine. There are, however, dangers in a malo-lactic fermentation, namely that the lactic bacteria found in wine falls into two groups: the safe ones which do not produce harmful by-products, or the hazardous ones that produce devastating results.

Only wines with a high acid content, which will protect them from spoilage bacteria, should undergo a malolactic fermentation. Wines with a pH of over 3.5 are at risk, and, in any case, it would be unnecessary to reduce their malic acid level. One of the spoilage bacteria, found in the group of lactic acid bacteria, can cause the malaise 'ROPINESS'. The bacteria hangs together in strings or rods, gives a shiny viscous appearance, and when poured has an oil-like viscosity. Another strain of the bacteria has been attributed to the production of 'MANNITOL'. The bacteria attack the fructose in the wine, reducing it to mannitol, which is very bitter and it cannot be corrected or removed. It is therefore important that sweet wines do not undergo a malolactic fermentation.

Another disorder, 'Tourne', is also associated with the bacteria that attack the tartaric acid, giving a sour, mousy odour and insipid taste. Winemakers describe this by the term 'MOUSENESS'. Mousy wines have also been associated with the decomposition of yeast cells and other insoluble matter which has dropped to the bottom of the jar, known as the 'lees'. These dead yeast cells will start to autolyse if left for a long time, and will release trace elements that encourage the growth of bacteria.

These problems all sound ominous, but there are only a few simple rules to adhere to for preventing their development. Rack the wine when a heavy deposit forms, maintain acid and sulphite levels and keep the finished wine in a cool place.

Acetification

Wines affected by bacteria that rely on oxygen (aerobic) can rarely be saved when in an advanced stage. The 'Wine to Vinegar' is undoubtedly the most common and is caused by the aerobic bacteria called 'ACETOBACTERS'. It infects the wine by using the oxygen present to convert some of the alcohol and sugar into acetic acid. Small amounts of acetic acid are natural constituents that occur in wine during fermentation. The bacteria that cling to the fruit, or winery equipment, and can be carried by the little vinegar flies, will develop if left exposed to the air. In the early stages a light film or veil forms on the surface of the wine and produces an acrid smell, which develops to a pronounced vinegar smell. Unless detected in the early stages, very little can be done to save it. In practise, preventive measures must be taken. Acetic bacteria need air in order to develop, so it can be prevented by keeping the container full, fitted with a protective airlock and by sterilising all winemaking equipment. When wine is bottled keep the air space to an absolute minimum.

Flowers of wine (Fleur)

This infection is caused by an aerobic yeast which has the ability to grow when the main alcohol fermentation has ceased. It becomes apparent by a thin whitish growth which appears on the surface of the wine. As it grows and thickens, it will cover the whole surface and as the yeast develops by feeding on the alcohol and the organic acids, it will give the wine a vapid, objectionable flavour. The exclusion of air and the use of sulphite will prevent an infection, but if detected at an early stage, the wine can be saved. It is advisable to rack the infected wine into a clean jar or container, keeping the siphon tube below the surface film to prevent any being carried into the clean jar. Add 2 crushed Campden tablets or 10 ml (2 tsp) of strong sulphite solution to each 4.5-litre demijohn, and ensure the jar is full by adding some wine or water to exclude the air.

Metallic hazes

These occur only if the must or wine have been in contact with any metal other than stainless steel. A common cause of this problem is the use of tinned ingredients when the tin has been damaged and the protective inner seal broken. In this case a whitish tint appears in white wines and a metallic blue tint in red wines. The addition of 5 grams of citric acid per gallon of wine will usually prevent further development of the problem, but the haze will not disperse and the wine should be filtered.

The list of potential problems may appear alarming, but you will only occasionally meet any of them if you take heed of the basic principles:

1. *Ensure cleanliness of utensils at all times*
2. *Use only high quality ingredients*
3. *Take care to prevent oxidation in must and wine*
4. *Use sulphite as necessary (Campden tablets or sodium or potassium metabisulphite)*
5. *Maintain acid levels*
6. *Check temperature, chemical additives (pectin-destroying enzymes, nutrients) and sugar during fermentation*
7. *Use only plastic or stainless steel containers for preparation and glass for storage*
8. *Rack as soon as a heavy deposit appears*
9. *Top up storage jars*

Wine Tasting

Each person with the ability to taste has their own preferences and prejudices, and this can frequently influence their judgement.

Wine tasting can be a very simple or an extremely complex art. One allows the novice to decide which he prefers and enjoys; the connoisseur with wide experience and 'taste memory' will detect the crucial balance when all characteristics should harmonise. Not only will he be able to detect the four main senses, between acidity, bitter, sweet and salty, but the classification of the vineyard and the style and quality of cellar craft during its production.

There are many pitfalls in wine tasting – the taster's physical condition, a bad cold, medication, a digestive disorder or fatigue will impair the entire olfactory system. An astringent or harsh wine will often influence the taster's impression of the next wine. Smell will give a good indication if wines are young, mature, fruity, homogeneous, clean, corked or musty.

We have become accustomed to adjectives and phrases used on some television programmes which border on the ridiculous, and even the jargon used by professional wine tasters may seem bizarre or ostentatious. Many of the terms used help to describe the character of the wine and should give an accurate indication of expected bouquet and aroma. The dedicated winemaker will, with practise, be able to identify the following terms and build up a 'taste memory' of many of them.

Acetic	Vinegary
Acid	Sharp taste
Aroma	Fruity smell
Astringent	A dry, mouth puckering effect
Austere	Severe, undeveloped
Balanced	A harmonious equilibrium between sweetness, acidity, tannin, alcohol, etc.
Big	A full flavoured wine
Bitter	Stinging taste perceptible in the aftertaste
Body	The content of fruit extract in the wine
Bottle age	Mellowing effect of years spent in bottle

Bouquet	The perfume or aroma of the wine
Brilliance	Clarity
Clean	Without any 'off' aroma or taste
Cloying	A sweet, heavy wine, lacking acidity
Coarse	Rough texture
Common	Lacking quality and maturity
Complex	Scents within scents
Corky	Mouldy taint
Dead	Old wine which has faded
Delicate	Charm and balance
Distinguished	With exceptional character
Dry	Absence of residual sugar
Dull	Uninteresting, probably insipid
Earthy	Overtones derived from soils
Elegant	Stylish balance and refinement of quality
Fine	Superior quality
Finish	End taste and last impression
Flat	Dull, insipid
Flinty	A hint of gunflint in bouquet and flavour
Flowery	Fragrant, flower-like
Foxy	A distinctive tang relating to native American vine spices
Fresh	Young wine with charm and vitality
Fruity	Wines with good fruit content
Green	Raw, often produced with immature fruit
Harsh	Coarse, rough and astringent
Heavy	Over endowed with alcohol and extract
Homogenous	Completely blended
Legs or tears	Trails that slide down the inside of a glass after swirling the wine
Length	The time various tastes remain with the drinker
Lemon	Overtones of lemon caused by excess citric acid
Maderised	Over mature and slightly oxidised
Mouldy	Undesirable flavour often developed from storage vessels
Noble	Indicates quality
Nose	Combined smell of bouquet and aroma
Oaky	Kept too long in contact with oak barrel or chips
Off	Unclean, tainted
Penetrating	Has physical effect on the nostrils
Petillant	Causing a prickly sensation in the mouth
Powerful	Self-explanatory attribution to some red wines
Ripe	Having reached its maturity plateau
Robe	A term used to describe the colour of the wine
Robust	Full-bodied
Rounded	A smooth feeling as the wine passes over the palate
Short	The taste remains for only a little while
Sick	Diseased, out of condition
Small	A wine of little consequence

Soft	Mellow
Sour	On the way to becoming vinegary
Spicy	Herb like, a characteristic of the Gewürztraminer grape
Stalky	Harshness caused by excessive pressing or fermentation of unripe stalks
Sulphury	A whiff of sulphur in young wines
Sweet	A wine with a high sugar content
Tart	Over acid
Thin	Watery, lacking body
Velvety	Smooth wine and often has a high glycerol content
Volatile	An unstable wine
Yeasty	Retaining the odour of yeast

$\mathcal{OS}$ERVING WINE

THERE IS ALWAYS an air of expectancy in selecting and opening a bottle of wine; if it has been made and stored correctly, this will be confirmed when the cork is pulled.

Choosing the right type of wine for the occasion is an art in itself. First make sure that the wine is fully matured. The light flower and low-acid wines can be drunk when they are no more than six months old, while the average fruit wine will need at least twelve months. Young red wines are often harsh owing to their high tannin content and, except for wines that were pasteurised in the preparation stage, will need at least one or two years to mature. The full-bodied deep reds take several years to mellow and improve in character. The high tannin content improves the keeping qualities of these wines and they will remain in peak condition for several years. Dessert wines, owing to their high fruit and acid content, will also need to be stored for at least two years. It is often said that the last bottle in the batch is the best.

Expertise in presenting your wine will enhance its appeal, whatever the occasion. If you are giving a dinner party, it is usual to start with a light white wine, which will not cloy the palate, thus obscuring the lightness of the first course. White wines are best served cool, about 10 °C (50 °F), but they should not be over-chilled or they will lose some of their flavour and bouquet. As the meal proceeds, heavier white or red wines will complement

the food. Red wines should be served at room temperature, about 18–20 °C (65–70 °F). If a quality wine has been stored for a long period, it should be decanted, as this not only ensures that the wine is free from any sediment but allows it to 'breathe' – i.e. to absorb oxygen which reacts with the wine, enhancing its flavour and bouquet. The length of time the wine should be left in the decanter varies, but generally the lighter red wines will need about half an hour and the full-bodied reds an hour. Well-made sweet wines can be enchanting and complement the dessert course, but for cheese it is better to stay with the reds.

At a social gathering the medium dry white and red wines are popular, and these too will be enhanced if served at the correct temperature as described above. For a wine to be drunk on its own it must be good, but no matter how much care you have taken, there will always be the lesser wines. These are suitable for drinking as everyday family wines, or if the alcoholic strength is adequate, they make a good base for a party punch, when flavourings and herbs will mask their lesser qualities.

The type of glasses chosen for serving wine plays an important part. Plain clear glasses are preferable, as coloured and heavily engraved glasses distract attention from the wine. Make sure the glasses are sparkling clean so that when the wine is poured it reflects its true clarity and colour. Wine glasses should preferably be generous in size so that they are only filled to two-thirds of their capacity. This allows the bouquet to develop on top of the wine. For sparkling wines tall flute-type glasses are the best, as this shape will slow down the release of the tiny bubbles of carbon dioxide caused by the decomposition of ethyl pyrocarbonate.

Whatever the occasion – family anniversaries, parties with friends, summer outings and barbecues or cold winter's evenings by the fire – it will unfailingly be enriched by sharing a bottle of home-made wine.

ASIC WINE-MAKING TECHNIQUES FOR BEGINNERS

IF YOU HAVE NEVER made wine before, it is a good idea to make a practical start using one of the grape concentrates, and as the process of fermentation gets underway, the techniques described in other sections of the book will be more readily understood.

You will need to buy a few simple items of equipment. The basic requirements are:

Two glass demijohns
One plastic white bucket with lid
A bored bung with an airlock
A bung to seal the demijohn when fermentation ceases
A plastic funnel and sieve
A piece of plastic tubing about 2 metres (6 feet) long
Wine bottles and corks
1 tin or carton of grape concentrate
1 bottle of Campden tablets
1 bottle or tub of pectin-destroying enzyme
1 bottle of vitamin B$_1$ tablets
Yeast nutrient
Wine yeast

If you do not wish to purchase the necessary chemicals at this stage, you will be able to purchase a 'boxed grape wine kit', which will include all the necessary ingredients and chemicals to make a 4.5-litre demijohn of wine, with full day-to-day instructions.

Other utensils necessary, such as a wooden or stainless steel spoon and a Pyrex measuring jug, are usually to be found in the kitchen.

First the yeast must be activated. Wash a small bottle (about 284 ml/ ^{1}/$_2$ pint in size) and sterilise by boiling it for 15 minutes. Cool and half fill the bottle with cooled boiled water, add the juice of half a lemon (25 ml) and 10 g (2 tsp) of sugar. Shake the mixture well and add 1 tablet or a sachet of wine yeast. Plug the top of the bottle with cotton wool and leave in a warm place (about 18–20 °C/65–70 °F). After 24 hours, bubbles should be rising rapidly to the surface as the yeast colony builds up.

Now prepare the demijohn by washing it thoroughly and draining. Crush 2 Campden tablets in 568 ml (1 pint) of tepid water and pour into the demijohn. Place a bung in position and shake the jar well so that the liquid covers the inside of the jar; leave for 15 minutes. Remove the bung, place it with the airlock and funnel in a bowl and pour the Campden tablet

starter bottle

solution over them. Wash the demijohn thoroughly with cold water to remove any traces of the Campden solution.

Half fill the demijohn with cold boiled water and empty in the contents of the tin of grape concentrate. Swirl the liquid to distribute the concentrate evenly and pour in the active yeast starter. Plug fairly tightly with cotton wool. After 24 hours the fermentation should be quite active. Many of the grape concentrates contain the correct amount of sugar, others need the addition of sugar; if this addition is necessary, when the fermentation is

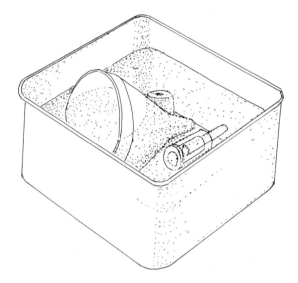

airlock, funnel and bung in sterilising solution

very active dissolve the required amount of sugar in 1 litre (1³/₄ pints) of water and pour into the demijohn. The jar at this stage should be seven-eighths full. The airlock should now be pushed into the holed bung and a little Campden tablet solution added to the airlock to ensure a good seal. Push the bung tightly into the neck of the demijohn and stand this in a warm place. As the yeast colony builds up, the liquid will become more cloudy and the released gas bubbles will push their way through the airlock, causing a rapid popping sound. When the first vigorous fermentation subsides (usually after about three days) the demijohn should be topped up with cold boiled water. After about two weeks the fermentation will gradually decrease, and you will notice the slowing down of the bubbles passing through the airlock until finally they cease altogether. The wine should then be racked following the instructions on page 25.

After you have made your first few grape concentrate wines, the next step is wines made from fruit juices. These can easily be purchased from shops and supermarkets. Make sure they are juices and not 'like juice'. The

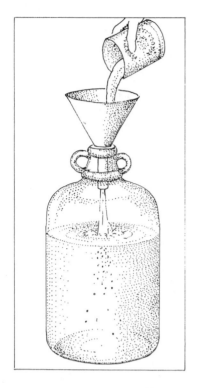
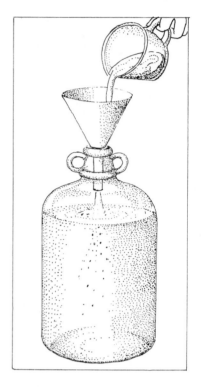

pour grape concentrate into
boiled water and add yeast

add sugar syrup after 24 hours

choices are considerable, and although orange is the most common, non-citrus fruits are more successful, although small quantities of orange juice can be included. The acidity and sweetness of the juice are fairly uniform. Grape juices are considerably higher in sugar but on their own these carton juices tend to make a rather bland wine, especially the white juice, which does not retain its fresh clean character and is more useful for blending with more positive flavours.

Some of the juices do create an excessive amount of frothing in the early stages of fermentation. This is because small particles of fruit are in the juice, so it is advisable to strain them through a fine muslin or nylon cloth to remove any particles of fruit before using. It will prove interesting to compile some of your own combinations after gaining a little experience. If possible, include 1 litre (1¾ pints) of grape juice, which will provide the essential tartaric acid that is lacking in the stone fruit varieties.

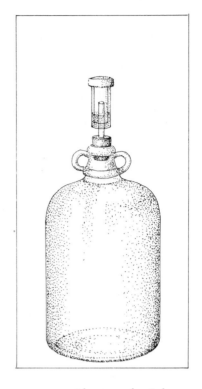

fit airlock   *top up with water after 3 days*

EASY RECIPES FOR BEGINNERS

PEACH, APRICOT AND APPLE

2 x 1 litre cartons (3½ pints) blended peach, apricot and orange juice
1 litre carton (1¾ pints) grape juice
1 litre carton (1¾ pints) apple juice
450 g (1 lb) sugar
Water to 4.5 litres (1 gal.)

10 g (2 tsp) pectin-destroying enzyme
5 g (1 tsp) yeast nutrient
All-purpose wine yeast
Campden tablets

Activate the yeast starter bottle (see page 17)
Sterilise all equipment as required
Start records

STAGE 1: Strain the juices through a fine muslin or nylon cloth to remove any fruit particles and pour into the demijohn. Add the pectin-destroying enzyme and yeast nutrient. In many recipes it is necessary to add a vitamin B$_1$ tablet, but I found it unnecessary to add to the fruit juices. Add the yeast from the starter bottle and stand the jar in a warm place, 18–21 °C

43

(65–70 °F); plug the top of the jar with cotton wool, which will encourage the fermentation to start quickly. After 24 hours replace with an airlock. We now refer to the juices as must. When the vigorous fermentation subsides, pour some of the must into a large jug and add the sugar. When dissolved, return to the demijohn; if frothing occurs leave for a few days before topping up with water. The fermentation should last about a fortnight. When it ceases, the wine should be racked following the instructions on page 25.

CRANBERRY AND BLACKCURRANT

2 x 1 litre cartons (3^{1}/$_{2}$ pints) cranberry and blackcurrant juice
1 litre carton (1^{3}/$_{4}$ pints) red grape juice
1 litre carton (1^{3}/$_{4}$ pints) apple juice
450 g (1 lb) sugar
Water to 4.5 litres (1 gal.)

10 g (2 tsp) pectin-destroying enzyme
5 g (1 tsp) yeast nutrient
All purpose wine yeast
Campden tablets

Activate the yeast starter bottle
Sterilise all equipment as required
Start records

Proceed as in *Peach, Apricot and Apple, Stage 1.*

FRESH FRUIT JUICE

1 litre carton (1^{3}/$_{4}$ pints)
Tropicano fresh mixed fruit juices
2 x 1 litre cartons (3^{1}/$_{2}$ pints)
fresh apple juice
600 g (1 lb 5oz) sugar
Water to 4.5 litres (1 gal.)

10 g (2 tsp) pectin-destroying enzyme
5 g (1 tsp) yeast nutrient
All purpose wine yeast
Campden tablets

Activate the yeast starter bottle
Sterilise all equipment as required
Start records

Proceed as in *Peach, Apricot and Apple, Stage 1.*

This wine is much more expensive to make and has been limited to 3 litres (5^{1}/$_{4}$ pints) of fresh juice instead of 4 litres (7 pints) in the first two, but it makes a far superior wine.

RECIPES

CERTAIN POINTS and procedures relevant to all the wines within a section are given in detail only in the first recipe of that section; these are printed in bold so that they may be easily referred to.

Quantities are given in metric and imperial measurements throughout the recipe pages. A full conversion table may be found on page 148. The metric or imperial volumes given for flowers represents as many petals (without the calyx and stalk) as will fit comfortably into a jug of the relevant capcity.

All recipes are for making 4.5 litres (1 gal.) of wine. Larger quantities should be made to the same proportions.

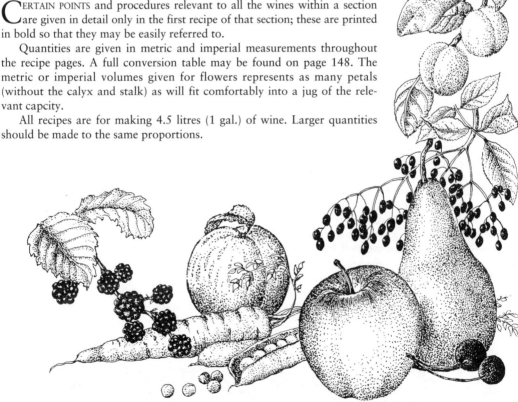

FLOWER WINES

ALTHOUGH FLOWER WINES are often frowned upon, they can be delightful if the flowers are used in the right proportions. Flowers on their own make a rather thin, insipid wine with an overpowering bouquet, but if they are used in conjunction with other carefully selected ingredients, their contribution both in aroma and flavour transforms an ordinary wine into something unique. The type of flowers used will depend largely on where you live. One of the nicest and most easily obtainable is elderflower. It is important to select the pale cream or white variety and not the heavy clusters of deep creamy flowers which impart a 'catty' bouquet to the wine.

Rose petals are usually in plentiful supply and the quantity required can be gathered quickly, preferably on a fine sunny morning when the flowers are in full bloom. It is a good idea to gather petals from more than one variety of rose, limiting the quantity of the heavily scented ones.

Any list of flowers for winemaking would be incomplete without the dandelion. This is the flower traditionally used in winemaking by our grandparents, and the jokes about dandelion wine undoubtedly equal the music hall 'mother-in-law' ones of the mid-twentieth century. Pleasant wines can be made from dandelions, however, as long as the flowers are gathered in areas not affected by fumes from diesel lorries and cars, and the petals are stripped completely clear of all calyx and stalks.

Primroses have been frequently listed in flower recipes in the past. They grow in profusion in many areas but are now protected, so in view of this I have omitted them from the following recipes.

In using flowers the main aim is to impart a distinctive and pleasing bouquet to the wine and give delicacy and finesse to the flavour. Care must therefore be taken to prevent these qualities from being marred by using other ingredients with strong flavours. As the flowers will not contribute natural sugars, acids, tannins or nitrogenous substances, fruits must be selected to fill the gap. As these wines are light with a refined elegance, it is important that the supporting fruit should not have a dominating flavour. Apple, gooseberry, grape juice, grape concentrate or white Australian sultanas are the perfect medium for white wines. Redcurrants, cherries or rosé grape concentrate are ideal in making wines from rose petals. The fruits will supply what is lacking in the flowers, adding vinosity and flavour, qualities that make a wine rather than an alcoholic beverage.

There are two methods of making this wine successfully. The first and easiest way is to infuse the flowers in the fermenting must. When the fermentation in the demijohn is under way, select the flowers – preferably on a fine sunny day after the dew has risen but before the sun dries out the volatile oils. Remove any green calyx or stalks and lightly wash the florets before placing them in a loose nylon or muslin bag. Tie with a strong piece of cotton, leaving long ends so the bag can be suspended in the fermenting must. Each day remove the airlock and give the cotton attachment a few vigorous jerks to distribute the flavour. After two or three days, depending on the strength of the florets' bouquet, remove the bag from the must. It is important not to let the florets remain for more than a few days, as prolonged fermentation on them can produce a slight bitterness.

The second method is suitable when using solid fruits, i.e. apples, cherries, gooseberries, sultanas or peaches, which are fermented on the pulp for two or three days. The florets can be included with the other ingredients at the beginning and will be strained out before the fermenting must is added to the demijohn. Do not boil or add boiling water to the petals, as the volatile substances will easily vaporise and be dissipated in the steam.

ELDERFLOWER 1
(grape concentrate)

Sulphite for sterilising: Dissolve 8 Campden tablets or 14 g of sodium or potassium metabisulphite in 1 litre (1³/4 pints) of water and store in a screw-topped bottle.

Strong sulphite solution to add to wines: Add 30 g (1 oz) sodium or potassium metabisulphite to 300 ml (¹/2 pint) of water. Store in a screw-topped bottle.

Yeast starter bottle: Sterilise a small bottle by boiling for 10 minutes or filling with sterilising sulphite and leaving 20 minutes. Pour back into the storage bottle and rinse twice to remove any sulphite solution. Half fill the bottle with cool boiled water, add the strained juice from half a lemon (25 ml), 10 g (2 tsp) granulated sugar and the wine yeast. Shake the bottle, plug with cotton wool and leave in a warm place (18–20 °C/65–70 °F) for 48 hours.

250 ml (9 fl oz) elderflower petals	5 g (1 tsp) pectin-destroying enzyme
1 litre (1³/4 pints) white grape concentrate	5 g (1 tsp) yeast nutrient
	1 vitamin B₁ tablet
226 g (¹/2 lb) sugar	Graves or Chablis type yeast
Water to 4.5 litres (1 gal.)	Campden tablets or strong sulphite solution

Activate the yeast starter bottle
Sterilise all equipment as required
Start records

Pour 3 litres (5¹/4 pints) of cold water to the bucket together with the pectin-destroying enzyme, yeast nutrient, vitamin B₁ tablet, grape concentrate and sugar. Stir all the ingredients until they are dissolved, pour into the demijohn with the yeast from the starter bottle, plugging the top with cotton wool. After 24 hours the fermentation should be active; if not, leave a few more hours.

STAGE 1: At this stage the flowers should be picked, removing any green calyx or stalks, washed carefully in cold water and placed in a nylon or muslin bag securely tied and suspended into the demijohn, making sure that the ends of the cotton hang from the top of the demijohn. Put a little sulphite solution in the airlock to ensure a good seal, and fit to the top of the demijohn. Stand the demijohn in a warm place of 18–21 °C (65–70 °F) to ferment. Two or three times a day give the suspended bag some vigorous movement by pulling the cotton ends up and down to help release bouquet into the wine. Depending on the activity of the fermentation, the bag of florets should be removed after two or three days, as prolonged fermentation on the florets can produce a slight bitterness. When the nylon bag is removed, top up the jar with water.

STAGE 2: When the fermentation ceases (usually about two weeks) siphon the clearing wine from the sediment, and to ensure the wine clears quickly it will be necessary to add a fining agent, either bentonite or a simple and effective wine clearing kit (see pages 25–27 on Clearing). Move the wine to a cool place. After one or two days, rack again, adding 2 Campden tablets or 10 ml (2 tsp) of strong sulphite solution; top up with a little cold water and store in a cool place. After two weeks rack again, adding 1 more Campden tablet or 5 ml (1 tsp) of strong sulphite solution. Replace the air-lock with a cork bung. Rack again when a heavy deposit forms. Mature in bulk for 4 months.

Note: As you become familiar with a hydrometer, when the fermentation ceases a specific gravity reading can be taken. It should be below 1.000. If, however, the reading registers 0.990, this may be too dry for many palates, so it may be necessary to add a little sugar syrup after the final racking. Care must be taken not to add sulphite if the fermentation is still active, as the yeast enzymes will convert the sulphite to hydrogen sulphide. The wine must be racked off from the active yeast cells before adding sulphite.

ELDERFLOWER 2
(cold water infusion)

250 ml (9 fl oz) of elderflower petals
670 g (1 1/2 lb) white sultanas
1 kg (2 1/4 lb) mixed dessert apples
5 g (1 tsp) tartaric acid
560 g (1 1/4 lb) sugar
Water to 4.5 litres (1 gal.)

5 g (1 tsp) pectin destroying enzyme
5 g (1 tsp) yeast nutrient
1 vitamin B_1 tablet
Chardonnay or White Bordeaux
type yeast
2 g bentonite
Campden tablets or strong sulphate
solution

Activate the yeast starter bottle. See *Elderflower 1*
Sterilise all equipment as required. See *Elderflower 1*
Start records

Wash the apples and place in the deep freezer for 48 hours. Remove and place in a plastic bucket, adding 2.5 litres (4½ pints) of very hot water. As soon as the apples are soft, crush them with your hands and add the washed, chopped or lightly liquidised sultanas, the tartaric acid, pectin-destroying enzyme, yeast nutrient, vitamin B_1 tablet and 1 crushed Campden tablet or 5 ml (1 tsp) of strong sulphite solution. Stir well and securely cover with the fitted lid. Stir two or three times daily and after 48 hours strain the liquid through a strong muslin or nylon cloth. Leave for 12 hours for any debris to settle out before racking the clean liquid into another container. Add the sugar and yeast, pour into a fermentation demijohn and move to a warm place, 18–21 °C (65–70 °F). Plug with cotton wool and leave for 24 hours before fitting the airlock; to ensure a good seal, add a little sulphite solution to the airlock. When the fermentation is active pick the flowers and proceed as in **Elderflower 1, Stages 1 and 2**. As this recipe contains solid fruit, protein will be present, which can cause a haze. It is advisable to add a small quantity of bentonite to prevent this (see page 32 on Protein haze).

ELDERFLOWER 3
(pulp fermentation)

250 ml (9 fl oz) elderflowers	5 g (1 tsp) pectin-destroying enzyme
560 g (1¼ lb) white sultanas	5 g (1 tsp) yeast nutrient
340 g (12 oz) gooseberries	1 vitamin B_1 tablet
3 ripe bananas	Graves or White Bordeaux type yeast
560 g (1¼ lb) sugar	Campden tablets or strong sulphite
Water to 4.5 litres (1 gal.)	solution

Activate the yeast starter bottle. See *Elderflower 1*
Sterilise all equipment as necessary. See *Elderflower 1*
Start records

Wash the sultanas to remove all editable oil and chop or lightly liquidise; wash the gooseberries and then crush. Put in a white plastic bucket with 3 litres (5¼ pints) of cold water, 1 crushed Campden tablet or 5 ml (1 tsp) strong sulphite solution, the pectin-destroying enzyme, yeast nutrient, vitamin B_1 tablet and the freshly picked flower petals, making sure no green stalks or calyx are included. Thinly slice the peeled bananas and boil gently in 500 ml (18 fl oz) of water for 20 minutes, strain and add the cooled liquid into the fruit pulp. Stir, cover and leave for 24 hours. Add the yeast starter, carefully pouring to one side of the bucket to enable a colony of active yeast cells to become established before stirring into the bulk. After 24 hours the fermentation should be very active, forcing the fruit to the top of the liquid by the carbon dioxide released, forming a 'cap'. This should be broken up several times a day. After two days strain off the liquid through a fine muslin or nylon cloth and add the sugar; when dissolved pour into the fermentation jar, fitting an airlock and move to a warm place, 18–21 °C (65–70 °F). When the fermentation ceases, proceed as in **Elderflower 1, Stage 2**.

ELDERFLOWER 4
(fresh juice)

The development of orchard fresh apple juice over the past years has made it easily available and the quality of many local products is superb. It is preferable to obtain an organic one, which often has a very heavy sediment. After it has settled, the clear juice should be racked off from the sediment.

250 ml (9 fl oz) elderflower petals	5 g (1 tsp) pectin-destroying enzyme
3 litres (5¼ pints) English apple juice	5 g (1 tsp) yeast nutrient
340 g (12 oz) sugar	1 vitamin B₁ tablet
Water to 4.5 litres (1 gal.)	Graves or Chablis type yeast
	3 g of bentonite
	Campden tablets or strong sulphite solution

Activate the yeast starter bottle. *See Elderflower 1*
Sterilise all equipment as necessary. See *Elderflower 1*
Start records

Sterilise a white plastic bucket, funnel and airlock. Add the apple juice, sugar, pectin-destroying enzyme, yeast nutrient, vitamin B₁ tablet and the yeast. Stir until the sugar has thoroughly dissolved. Make the quantity up to 4.5 litres (1 gal.) with water. It is now possible to take an hydrometer reading in order to have a precise reading of the sugar present. To attain an alcoholic reading in the finished wine of 10.5% alcohol, the specific gravity of the liquid should be in the region of 1.080. If it has not reached the deserved level, which of course depends on the sweetness of the apple juice, a little more sugar can be added.

As a guide, 28 g (1 oz) of sugar will raise the SG in one litre by 0.010. Therefore if, for example, the SG reading has only reached an SG of 1.070 it will be necessary to add 126 g to a 4.5-litre demijohn:

$$4.5 \text{ litres} \times 28 \text{ g} = 126 \text{ g sugar}$$

When the sugar has been adjusted, pour into the demijohn, retaining 500 ml (18 fl oz) in a wine bottle, which will be poured into the demijohn later. When the first vigorous fermentation is active, proceed with **Elderberry 1, Stages 1 and 2**. The protein in the apple juice can cause a haze, so it is advisable to add a small quantity of bentonite to prevent it (see pages 25–27 on Clearing).

DANDELION
(pulp fermentation)

500 ml (18 fl oz) of dandelion petals
680 g (1¹/2 lb) white sultanas
3 oranges
5 g (1 tsp) malic acid
670 g (1¹/2 lb) sugar
Water to 4.5 litres (1 gal.)

5 g (1 tsp) pectin-destroying enzyme
5 g (1 tsp) yeast nutrient
1 vitamin B₁ tablet
Graves or White Bordeaux type yeast
Campden tablets or strong
sulphite solution

Activate the yeast starter bottle. See *Elderflower 1*
Sterilise all equipment as necessary. See *Elderflower 1*
Start records

Wash the sultanas to remove all edible oil and chop or lightly liquidise
in 2.5 litres (4¹/2 pints) of cold water. Add the juice from the oranges
and carefully skin the outside rind from one orange (avoiding taking any
white pith) and place in a white plastic bucket with the malic acid,
pectin-destroying enzyme, yeast nutrient, vitamin B₁ tablet, flower
petals and active yeast starter. Stir and replace the lid. As the fermentation becomes vigorous, the fruits will rise to the top of the liquid;
stir two or three times daily to break up the cap. After three days
strain, add the sugar and when dissolved pour into the demijohn, fitting the
airlock and move to a warm place. When fermentation ceases, proceed as in
Elderflower 1, Stage 2.

ROSE 1
(cold water infusion)

500 ml (18 fl oz) scented rose petals
670 g (1¹/2 lb) ripe peaches
1 litre (1³/4 pints) rosé or red grape juice
5 g (1 tsp) tartaric acid
400 g (14 oz) sugar
2 ripe bananas
Water to 4.5 litres (1 gal.)

5 g (1 tsp) pectin-destroying enzyme
5 g (1 tsp) yeast nutrient
1 vitamin B₁ tablet
Bordeaux type yeast
Campden tablets or strong sulphite
solution

Activate the yeast starter bottle. See *Elderflower 1*
Sterilise all equipment as necessary. See *Elderflower 1*
Start records

Wash and stone the peaches, crush them and place in a plastic bucket with
2.5 litres (4¹/2 pints) of water, 1 crushed Campden tablet or 5 ml (1 tsp) of
strong sulphite solution, tartaric acid, pectin-destroying enzyme and the vitamin B₁ tablet. Peel and thinly slice the bananas and boil for 10 minutes in
500 ml (18 fl oz) of water; strain the liquid from the bananas into the peach
pulp liquid. Stir and leave for 48 hours, stirring two or three times daily.
Strain through a double muslin or nylon cloth and leave until any heavy sediment sinks to the bottom of the container. Rack off the clean liquid and add

the sugar, yeast nutrient, grape juice and the active yeast starter. Stir well and pour into a 4.5-litre demijohn, filling the jar to seven-eighths full with water. Fit an airlock. A hydrometer reading can be taken at this stage; if the reading exceeds an SG of 1.080, when topping up the jar after a few days this should be with water. If, however, that is the exact reading, a weak syrup should be used for topping up the demijohn so the final alcoholic content is maintained. When the fermentation is active proceed as in **Elderflower 1, Stages 1 and 2.**

ROSE 2
(pulp fermentation)

500 ml (18 fl oz) rose petals	5 g (1 tsp) pectin-destroying enzyme
670 g (1½ lb) white sultanas	5 g (1 tsp) yeast nutrient
453 g (1 lb) mixed summer fruits (red or	1 vitamin B₁ tablet
white currants, gooseberries,	Bordeaux type yeast
raspberries)	Campden tablets or strong sulphite
450 g (1 lb) sugar	solution
Water to 4.5 litres (1 gal.)	2 g bentonite

Activate the yeast starter bottle. See *Elderflower 1*
Sterilise all equipment as necessary. See *Elderflower 1*
Start records

Wash the sultanas and mixed fruits, chop, crush or lightly liquidise before placing in a white plastic bucket with 3 litres (5¼ pints) of cold water. Add 1 crushed Campden tablet, the pectin-destroying enzyme, yeast nutrient, the flower petals lightly crushed, and the vitamin B₁ tablet. Stir well and replace the lid. After 24 hours add the yeast starter, carefully pouring to one side of the bucket to enable an active colony of yeast cells to become established before stirring into the bulk. After a further 24 hours the fermentation will be very active, forcing the fruit to the top of the liquid by carbon dioxide being released, forming a 'cap'. This should be broken up several times a day. After two days strain off the liquid through a fine muslin or nylon cloth and add the sugar. Pour into the demijohn, fit an airlock and move to a warm place, 18–21 °C (65–70 °F). After a few days top up the demijohn with a little cold water. It is advisable to add a small quantity of bentonite to stabilise any protein in the must (see page 32 on Protein haze). When the fermentation ceases, proceed as in **Elderflower 1, Stage 2.**

FRUIT WINES

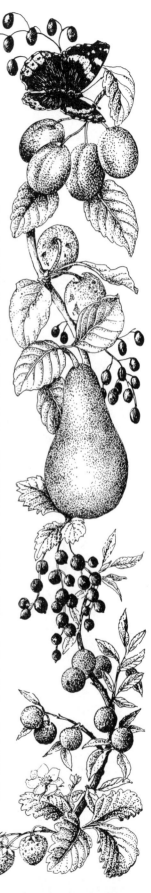

UNDOUBTEDLY FRUIT WINES will take pride of place over all others, for the quantity and variety of suitable fruits offer more scope than any other type. With so many differing acid levels, sugar quantities and flavours, the challenge for the winemaker is also greater: it enables one to prove one's expertise in producing well-balanced wines. Fruits forms the base for the whole range of types – aperitifs, dry table wines, medium sweet, dessert and sparkling wines. As the dry table and medium sweet wines are the most popular, most of the recipes will be of this type.

In our changing climate the seasons vary so considerably that each year's batch can range from vintage to non-vintage wine depending on the weather. During good summers the fruits contain a high proportion of sugars with less acid and in poor years the opposite applies. The winemaker should adjust his recipes slightly in the poor years by adding a little less of the acidic fruits but maintaining the body and quality of the wine by increasing the more bland ones. It is far better to blend the ingredients in the early stages so that they have time to harmonise, rather than blending the wines at a later stage.

The methods of fermentation are described fully on pages 10–11 but each method is described in detail in one of the recipes in each section. It should be remembered that fermentation on the pulp, provided that the top of the must is protected to exclude the oxygen, will give a greater rate of extraction of all the main ingredients: sugar, acids, tannins, flavour and nitrogenous substances. The infusion in water method will not give nearly such a high extraction rate but is more suitable for the lighter white table wines. Pasteurisation will extract colour, flavour and a medium proportion of acids and tannin but the wines made in this way are early maturing and lack the quality and character of the deep reds. This method serves a very useful purpose, however, as the wines can be drunk after twelve months, whereas the other reds take two or three years to mature, and should preferably be left for longer.

In selecting the fruits the emphasis must be on quality and ripeness. Undamaged fruits are useless if they are not fully ripe, for the sugar content will be low and the acids high; conversely fruits that are over-ripe with bacterial spoilage will rarely produce wines of great excellence. When picking wild fruits try to select areas free from heavy pollution and process the fruits as quickly as possible.

Some fruits present more problems than others to prepare; apples are particularly tricky owing to their fleshy nature. The simplest method is to use a juice extractor for small quantities or a fruit press for larger quantities (see pages 23–24). A little sulphite – 1 Campden tablet or 5 ml (1 tsp) of strong sulphite solution to every 3 kg (6½ lb) of fruit – will safeguard the juice from oxidation. An alternative method for almost all fruits is by cold

water infusion. The fruits are washed, drained and placed in a bag in the freezer for 48 hours. As ice crystals form, they break down the structures of the fruit and when thawed the juice will flow freely. As some fruits oxidise very quickly, they should be immediately processed. This applies particularly to apples, which can be frozen whole, and when removed from the freezer should be placed in a plastic bucket with 2 litres (3½ pints) of near boiling water poured over them.

In a short time the apples can be squashed by hand and it is important, at this stage, to add 1 Campden tablet or 5 ml (1 tsp) of strong sulphite solution to prevent oxidation. The availability of commercially produced fruit juices has helped reduce the task of juice extraction and is proving successful. It is important, however, to buy Fruit Juice and not cartons labelled 'Like Juice'.

Full instructions on pulp fermentation, juice extraction and cold water infusion after freezing are given in the first three fruit recipes, and reference can be made to these when following other fruit recipes.

Sultanas are recommended in many of the recipes; most sultanas are dipped in an edible mineral oil that should be removed by washing them carefully in warm water and draining before use. Recipes using bottled and canned fruits are also included; many of these wines will mature more quickly owing to their lower acid levels, so care must be taken to add the correct amount of sulphite at the end of the fermentation to protect them from bacterial infection.

Sweet wines need a higher proportion of sulphite than dry wines, as much of the sulphite is used up combining with sugars, acids and aldehydes to form bisulphite compounds that leave considerably reduced quantities of free sulphur dioxide to protect the wine from bacterial infection. Sorbic acid will control yeast growth in sweeter wines (see note on Sorbate on page 15).

APPLE 1
(pulp fermentation)

Sulphite for sterilising: Dissolve 8 Campden tablets or 14 g sodium or potassium metabisulphite in 1 litre (1³⁄4 pints) of cold water and store in a screw-topped bottle.

Strong sulphite solution for must and wine: Add 28 g (1 oz) to 500 ml (18 fl oz) of water. Store in a screw-topped bottle.

STAGE 1: Yeast starter bottle. Sterilise a small bottle either by boiling for 10 minutes or filling with the sterilising sulphite and leaving for 20 minutes. Pour back into the storage bottle and rinse twice with cold water. Half fill the bottle with cooled boiled water, add the juice from half a lemon (25 ml), 10 g (2 tsp) granulated sugar and the wine yeast. Shake the bottle, plug with cotton wool and leave in a warm place, 18–21 °C (65–70 °F), for 48 hours.

3 kg (6½ lb) mixed apples	10 g (2 tsp) pectin-destroying enzyme
453 g (1 lb) sultanas	5 g (1 tsp) yeast nutrient
566 g (1¼ lb) sugar	1 vitamin B₁ tablet
Water to 4.5 litres (1 gal.)	Hock type yeast
	Campden tablets or strong sulphite solution

STAGE 2: Sterilise all equipment as required
Start records

Place the utensils in the plastic bucket, pour in the sterilising solution.
Replace the lid tightly and swirl the solution around making sure that it
reaches all parts of the bucket. Leave for 20 minutes before returning the
solution to the storage bottle. It will remain effective for quite a long while
providing it retains its pungent odour. Carefully wash the bucket and
utensils with tap water to remove all traces of sulphite.

Dissolve 1 crushed Campden tablet or 5 ml (1 tsp) of strong sulphite
solution in 3 litres (5¼ pints) of cold water, placing in the sterilised fer-
menting bucket. Chop or slice the apples thinly and put them quickly into
the sulphited water to prevent them oxidising. Add the washed, chopped or
lightly liquidised sultanas, the pectin-destroying enzyme, yeast nutrient
and vitamin B₁ tablet. Stir and place an upturned plate on top of the fruit
to keep the fruit covered by liquid. Leave for 24 hours.

STAGE 3: Make sure the yeast starter is fully active before pouring it care-
fully into one side of the bucket. Reserve some in the starter bottle, topping
it up with a little cold water as a safeguard in case the bulk fails to activate.

If the active yeast starter is kept to a small area in the bucket, an active
yeast colony will quickly become established and can then be stirred into the
bulk must. When fully active, a fruit cap will form on the top of the must; this
should be kept submerged with an upturned dinner plate placed over the top
of the fruit, enabling a quicker and better extraction rate and excluding as
much oxygen as possible. The fruit cap should be broken up two or three
times daily. Ferment on the pulp for three days before straining off the liquid,
pressing the pulp lightly. Now add the sugar and pour into the demijohn.

STAGE 4: Increase level in the demijohn to only seven-eighths full, as some-
times excessive frothing may occur, thus wasting the must. Fit an airlock and
stand in a warm place, 18–21 °C (65–70 °F). When the vigorous fermentation
subsides, top up the demijohn with a little cold water. When the fermentation
ceases (usually two to three weeks), siphon the clearing wine from the sedi-
ment into a clean jar, replace the airlock and move to a cool place. After two
or three days siphon off the clear wine from the sediment again, adding 2
crushed Campden tablets or 10 ml (2 tsp) of strong sulphite solution. Store in
a cool place. Mature in bulk for 6 months.

Note: White wines with a high proportion of fruit often fail to clear owing
to protein held in suspension; as these carry a positive charge, many wine
makers will add a small quantity of the negatively charged bentonite,
which has the ability to combine with the protein and will fall out. This
can be added half way through the fermentation, or when fermentation
ceases a wine clearing kit can be used (see pages 25–27 on Clearing).

After two or three weeks the wines should be relatively clear; rack again, adding one more Campden tablet or 5 ml (1 tsp) of strong sulphite solution. Replace the airlock with a bung and store in a cool place. If a firm deposit settles on the bottom of the demijohn, rack once more and add 1 Campden tablet or 5 ml (1 tsp) of strong sulphite solution.

Note: If the finished wine has an SG reading of 0.990, this may be too dry for some palates. When a medium wine is preferred it is for the winemaker to decide if the wine would benefit by adding a little sugar syrup. The quantity of sugar required will be very minimal: 56 g (2 oz) will increase the SG by 0.005 in a 4.5-litre demijohn. If the SG reading at the end of the fermentation is 0.990, by adding 56 g an SG reading of 0.995 would be obtained. An ideal level for a table wine.

APPLE 2
(juice extraction)

1.5 litres ($2^3/_4$ pints) orchard fresh apple juice	10 g (2 tsp) pectin-destroying enzyme
426 ml ($^3/_4$ pint) white grape concentrate	5 g (1 tsp) yeast nutrient
453 g (1 lb) sugar	1 vitamin B_1 tablet
Water to 4.5 litres (1 gal.)	Hock or Chablis type yeast
	Campden tablets or strong sulphite solution

Activate the yeast starter bottle. See *Apple 1, Stage 1*
Sterilise all equipment as required. See *Apple 1, Stage 2*
Start records

When the yeast is active pour the apple juice into the bucket, add grape concentrate, pectin-destroying enzyme, yeast nutrient, vitamin B_1 tablet and the active yeast starter. Add enough water to increase the total liquid to 2.25 litres (4 pints).

STAGE 1: For those who wish to monitor the fermentation process, a hydrometer reading can be taken at this stage. If the quantity of liquid is below 2.25 litres (4 pints), increase with water to this level. Pour some of the liquid into the trial jar and insert the hydrometer. If the SG reading is 1.080 for half the quantity in a 4.5-litre demijohn, it must be divided (i.e. to 1.040) to give the SG reading for one 4.5-litre demijohn when filled with water at SG 1.000. In order to increase the SG level for a light white wine from SG 1.040 to SG 1.080 it will be necessary to raise the SG level by 0.040. From the SG table on page 147 it would require 482 g (1 lb 1 oz) of sugar to raise it to an SG level of 1.080. Red wines need more alcohol requiring extra sugar to reach an SG reading of 1.090.

STAGE 2: Pour all the must into a demijohn, adding an extra litre ($1^3/_4$ pints) of cold water, and plug the top with a piece of cotton wool. After 24 hours the fermentation should be active; the sugar required can then be dissolved in 750 ml ($1^3/_4$ pints) of hot water and added to the demijohn. Proceed as in Apple 1, Stage 4. Mature in bulk for 6 months.

APPLE 3

(Cold water infusion, freezing)

2 kg (4¹/₂ lb) of mixed dessert apples
1 kg (2¹/₂ lb) pears
453 g (1 lb) white sultanas
710 g (1 lb 9 oz) sugar
5 g (1 tsp) tartaric acid
Water to 4.5 litres (1 gal.)

10 g (2 tsp) pectin-destroying enzyme
5 g (1 tsp) yeast nutrient
1 vitamin B₁ tablet
Hock or Chablis type yeast
Campden tablets or strong sulphite
solution

Wash the required amount of apples and pears and place in the freezer for 48 hours.

Activate the yeast starter bottle. See *Apple 1, Stage 1*
Sterilise all equipment as required. See *Apple 1, Stage 2*
Start records

STAGE 1: Remove the frozen fruit from the freezer and place in the sterilised plastic bucket. Pour 2 litres (3¹/₂ pints) of near boiling water over the frozen fruit. In a short time the water will cool and the fruits can then be squashed by hand. Add 1 crushed Campden tablet or 5 ml (1 tsp) of strong sulphite solution, pectin-destroying enzyme, tartaric acid, yeast nutrient and vitamin B₁ tablet. Add the washed and chopped sultanas, stir well and cover with an upturned plate to keep the fruit well down in the liquid. Replace lid. Leave for three days, stirring the must two or three times daily. Strain, pressing the fruit, and pour into a demijohn and leave for 24 hours for the sedi-ment to sink to the bottom of the jar. Siphon back into the bucket, taking care no sediment is carried through. A hydrometer reading can be taken at this stage (see Apple 2, Stage 1*). Add the active yeast and sugar to the must; when dissolved, return to the demi-john, topping up to seven-eighths full with water. Proceed as in* Apple 1, Stage 4. *Mature in bulk for 6 months.*

APPLE 4

(pulp fermentation)

1.5 kg (3¹/₃ lb) crab apples
453 g (1 lb) fresh rosehips
720 g (1 lb 9¹/₂ oz) sugar
Water to 4.5 litres (1 gal.)

10 g (2 tsp) pectin-destroying enzyme
5g (1 tsp) yeast nutrient
1 vitamin B₁ tablet
Hock or Chablis type yeast
Campden tablets or strong sulphite
solution

Activate the yeast starter bottle. See *Apple 1, Stage 1*
Sterilise all equipment as required. See *Apple 1, Stage 2*
Start records

Crush the rosehips, finely chop or crush the crab apples and quickly place in the plastic bucket with 3 litres (5¼ pints) of cold water and 1 crushed Campden tablet or 5 ml (1 tsp) of strong sulphite solution. Add the washed and finely chopped sultanas, the pectin-destroying enzyme, yeast nutrient and vitamin B₁ tablet. Cover with a plate and leave for 24 hours. Add the active yeast starter and ferment on the pulp for three days, stirring the must two or three times daily to break up the fruit cap. Ensure the lid of the bucket is tightly secure at all times. Strain off the liquid and add the sugar, making sure it is fully dissolved before pouring into the demijohn. Proceed as in **Apple 1, Stage 4.**

Mature in bulk for 6 months before bottling.

APPLE 5
(juice extraction)

1 litre (1¾ pints) of Orchard fresh apple juice	5 g (1 tsp) pectin-destroying enzyme
500 ml (18 fl oz) of pineapple juice	5 g (1 tsp) yeast nutrient
3 ripe bananas	1 vitamin B₁ tablet
500ml (18 fl oz) white grape concentrate	White Bordeaux or Chardonnay type yeast
453g (1 lb) sugar	Campden tablets or strong sulphite solution
Water to 4.5 litres (1 gal.)	

Activate the yeast starter bottle. See *Apple 1, Stage 1*
Sterilise all equipment as required. See *Apple 1, Stage 2*
Start records

Boil the peeled, thinly sliced bananas in 500 ml (18 fl oz) of water for 20 minutes; drain off the liquid, discarding the pulp. When cool add the apple juice, pineapple juice, grape concentrate, pectin-destroying enzyme, yeast nutrient, vitamin B₁ tablet and active yeast starter. An SG reading can be taken at this stage (see **Apple 2, Stage 1**). Pour into the demijohn, top up to three-quarters full with cold water and plug the top with cotton wool. When the fermentation is active the dissolved sugar may be added. Proceed as in **Apple 1, Stage 4.**

Mature in bulk for 6 months before bottling. Store in a cool place.

APRICOT 1
(cold water infusion)

720 g (1 lb 9½ oz) fresh apricots	5 g (1 tsp) yeast nutrient
453 g (1 lb) white sultanas	1 vitamin B₁ tablet
3 ripe bananas	Hock or White Chardonnay type yeast
5 g (1 tsp) tartaric acid	Campden tablets or strong sulphite solution
720 g (1 lb 9½ oz) sugar	
Water to 4.5 litres (1 gal.)	
5 g (1 tsp) pectin-destroying enzyme	

Activate the yeast starter bottle. See *Apple 1, Stage 1* **Sterilise all equipment as required. See** *Apple 1, Stage 2*
Start records

Add 1 crushed Campden tablet or 5 ml (1 tsp) strong sulphite solution to 1.75 litres (3 pints) of cold water. Stone the apricots, discarding the stones, and finely slice. Wash and chop or lightly liquidise the sultanas and add to the liquid. Boil the peeled, thinly sliced bananas in 500 ml (18 fl oz) of water for 20 minutes, adding the strained liquid with the pectin-destroying enzyme, yeast nutrient, tartaric acid and vitamin B$_1$ tablet, and stir well. Keep the fruit pulp submerged with a plate and the bucket tightly covered. Leave for three days, stirring the must two or three times daily. Strain, pressing the fruit, and pour into a demijohn and leave for 24 hours for the sediment to settle to the bottom of the jar. Siphon the clear liquid back into the bucket. A hydrometer reading can be taken at this stage (see **Apple 2, Stage 1**). Dissolve the sugar in 1 litre (1^3/$_4$ pints) of water and add to the must with the yeast starter. Pour into the demijohn and fit an airlock. Proceed as in **Apple 1, Stage 4**.

Mature in bulk for 6 months before bottling. Store in a cool place.

APRICOT 2
(pulp fermentation)

2 medium sized tins of apricots (1.1 kg/2 lb 7 oz)
1 litre (1^3/$_4$ pints) of apple juice
4 ripe bananas
600 g (1^1/$_3$ lb) white sultanas
5 ml (1 tsp) tartaric acid
600 g (1^1/$_3$ lb) sugar
500 ml (18 fl oz) cream or yellow rose petals
Water to 4.5 litres (1 gal.)

10 g (2 tsp) pectin-destroying enzyme
5 g (1 tsp) yeast nutrient
1 vitamin B$_1$ tablet
Sauternes type yeast
Campden tablets or strong sulphite solution

Activate the yeast starter bottle. See *Apple 1, Stage 1*
Sterilise all equipment as required. See *Apple 1, Stage 2*
Start records

Boil the peeled sliced bananas in 1 litre (1^3/$_4$ pints) of water for 20 minutes and strain the liquid into a white plastic bucket. Add the apple juice, apricots, tartaric acid, pectin-destroying enzyme, yeast nutrient, vitamin B$_1$ tablet, rose petals and washed, finely chopped sultanas. Pour in the active yeast starter. Proceed as in **Apple 1, Stages 3 and 4.**

Mature in bulk for 6 months before bottling. Store in a cool place.

APRICOT 3

(cold water infusion, freezing)

1 kg (2¹/₄ lb) fresh apricots	5 g (1 tsp) pectin-destroying enzyme
453 g (1 lb) gooseberries	5 g (1 tsp) yeast nutrient
600 g (1¹/₃ lb) white sultanas	1 vitamin B₁ tablet
710 g (1 lb 9 oz) sugar	Hock or Chablis type yeast
Water to 4.5 litres (1 gal.)	Campden tablets or strong sulphite
	solution

Wash the apricots and gooseberries and place in the freezer for 48 hours.

Activate the yeast starter bottle. See *Apple 1, Stage 1*
Sterilise all equipment as required. See *Apple 1, Stage 2*
Start records

Remove the frozen fruit from the freezer and place in a white plastic bucket.
Pour 2 litres (3¹/₂ pints) of near boiling water over the fruit. In a short time
the water will cool and the fruits can be quickly squashed by hand. Add
1 crushed Campden tablet or 5 ml (1 tsp) of strong sulphite solution, the
washed, chopped or lightly liquidised sultanas, pectin-destroying enzyme,
yeast nutrient and vitamin B₁ tablet. Stir well and cover with an upturned
plate to ensure the fruits are covered by liquid. Replace lid. Leave for three
days, stirring the must two or three times daily. Strain, pressing the fruit,
and pour into a demijohn; leave for 24 hours for the sediment to sink to the
bottom of the demijohn. Siphon off the clear liquid into a bucket. A
hydrometer reading can be taken at this stage (see **Apple 2, Stage 1**).
Dissolve the sugar in 1 litre (1³/₄ pints) of cold water and add to the must
with the active yeast starter. Pour back into the demijohn and fit an airlock.
Proceed as in **Apple 1, Stage 4**.
　　Mature in bulk for 6 months before bottling.

BILBERRY

(pasteurised)

1 kg (2¹/₂ lb) bilberries or 2 x 568 ml	5 g (1 tsp) pectin-destroying enzyme
(1 pint) jars of bilberries	5 g (1 tsp) yeast nutrient
453 g (1 lb) sloes or bullaces	1 vitamin B₁ tablet
284 g (10 oz) dried currants	Burgundy type yeast
453 g (1 lb) sultanas	Campden tablet or strong sulphite
600 g (1¹/₃ lb sugar	solution
Water to 4.5 litres (1 gal.)	

Activate the yeast starter bottle. See *Apple 1, Stage 1*
Sterilise all equipment as required. See *Apple 1, Stage 2*
Start records

Wash the sloes or bullaces and place in a stainless steel saucepan with 2.5 litres (4½ pints) of water. Heat to 65 °C (150 °F), maintaining the temperature for 5 minutes. When cool pour into a white plastic bucket. Wash the currants and sultanas, chop or very lightly liquidise and add with the bilberries to the fruit. Add the pectin-destroying enzyme, yeast nutrient, vitamin B₁ tablet and yeast starter, and cover with an upturned plate and replace lid. Ferment on the pulp for three days, stirring two or three times daily to break up the fruit cap, which will rise to the top of the must. Strain the liquid into another container before adding the sugar. When dissolved pour into the demijohn, topping up with water. Proceed as in **Apple 1, Stage 4.**

Mature in bulk for 6 months before bottling. As this wine has been partially pasteurised, it will mature quite quickly for a red wine.

BLACKBERRY 1
(pulp fermentation)

1 kg (2½ lb) blackberries	5 g (1 tsp) pectin-destroying enzyme
600 g (1⅓ lb) sloes, bullaces or blackcurrants	5 g (1 tsp) yeast nutrient
600 g (1⅓ lb) sultanas	1 vitamin B₁ tablet
710 g (1 lb 9 oz) sugar	Burgundy type yeast
Water to 4.5 litres (1 gal.)	Campden tablets or strong sulphite solution

Activate the yeast starter bottle. See *Apple 1, Stage 1*
Sterilise all equipment as required. See *Apple 1, Stage 2*
Start records

Wash and crush the blackberries and sloes, wash and chop the sultanas and place in a white plastic bucket with 3 litres (5¼ pints) of cold water, 1 crushed Campden tablet or 5 ml (1 tsp) of strong sulphite solution, the pectin-destroying enzyme, yeast nutrient and vitamin B₁ tablet. Cover and leave for 24 hours before adding the yeast starter. Ferment on the pulp for three days, keeping the fruit submerged with an upturned plate and the bucket tightly covered. Stir two or three times daily to break up the fruit cap. After three days strain off the liquid through a fine muslin or nylon cloth and add the sugar. When dissolved, pour into a demijohn. Proceed as in **Apple 1, Stage 4.**

Mature in bulk for 6 months before bottling. Owing to extra acidity, alcohol and more body, this wine will need maturing in bottle for another 12 months.

BLACKBERRY 2

(cold water infusion, freezing)

1 kg (2¼ lb) blackberries	5 g (1 tsp) pectin-destroying enzyme
1 kg (2¼ lb) apples	5 g (1 tsp) yeast nutrient
1 kg (2¼ lb) pears	1 vitamin B_1 tablet
526 ml (19 fl oz) red grape concentrate	Burgundy type yeast
600 g (1⅓ lb) sugar	Campden tablets or strong sulphite
Water to 4.5 litres (1 gal.)	solution

Wash the blackberries, removing any debris, the apples and pears and place in the freezer for 48 hours.

Activate the yeast starter bottle. See *Apple 1, Stage 1*
Sterilise all equipment as required. See *Apple 1, Stage 2*
Start records

Remove the frozen fruit from the freezer and place in a white plastic bucket. Pour 2.5 litres (4½ pints) of near boiling water over the fruit. In a short time the fruit will thaw, at which point it can be squashed by hand. Add 1 crushed Campden tablet or 5 ml (1 tsp) of strong sulphite solution, the yeast nutrient, pectin-destroying enzyme and vitamin B_1 tablet. Stir well and cover with an upturned plate to ensure the fruits are covered by the liquid. Replace lid. Leave for three days, stirring the must twice daily. Strain, pressing the fruit, and pour into the demijohn; leave for 24 hours for the sediment to settle before siphoning the clear liquid back into the bucket. A hydrometer reading can be taken at this stage (see **Apple 2, Stage 1**). *Note*: For this heavier wine an SG reading of 1.090 is necessary. Proceed as in **Apple 1, Stage 4**.

Mature in bulk for 6 months before bottling. The wine needs maturing in bottle.

BLACKBERRY 3

(pasteurised)

1 kg (2¼ lb) blackberries	5 g (1 tsp) pectin-destroying enzyme
453 g (1 lb) elderberries	5 g (1 tsp) yeast nutrient
4 ripe bananas	1 vitamin B_1 tablet
5 g (1 tsp) tartaric acid	Burgundy type yeast
284 ml (½ pint) red grape concentrate	Campden tablets or strong sulphite
800 g (1¾ lb) sugar	solution
Water to 4.5 litres (1 gal.)	

Activate the yeast starter bottle. See *Apple 1, Stage 1*
Sterilise all equipment as required. See *Apple 1, Stage 2*
Start records

De-stalk and wash the elderberries and blackberries, crush and place in a stainless steel saucepan adding 1.5 litres (2¾ pints) of cold water. Heat to 65 °C (150 °F); maintain this heat for 5 minutes.

Boil the peeled, sliced bananas in 500 ml (18 fl oz) of water for 20 minutes, adding the strained liquid to the other ingredients in a white plastic bucket. When cool add tartaric acid, pectin-destroying enzyme, yeast nutrient and vitamin B₁ tablet. Stir well and leave for 24 hours before straining off the liquid and lightly pressing the pulp. A hydrometer reading can be taken at this stage (see **Apple 2, Stage 1**).

Dissolve the sugar in 1 litre (1¾ pints) of water, add this and the red grape concentrate to the liquid and pour into the demijohn with the yeast starter. Plug the top of the jar with cotton wool and as soon as the fermentation becomes active fit an airlock. Proceed as in **Apple 1, Stage 4**.

Mature in bulk for 3 months before bottling.

BLACKCURRANT
(pulp fermentation)

680 g (1½ lb) blackcurrants	5 g (1 tsp) pectin-destroying enzyme
453 g (1 lb) dried currants	5 g (1 tsp) yeast nutrient
226 g (½ lb) sultanas	1 vitamin B₁ tablet
4 ripe bananas	Burgundy or Rhone type yeast
800g (1¾ lb) sugar	Campden tablets or strong sulphite
Water to 4.5 litres (1 gal.)	solution

Activate the yeast starter bottle. See *Apple 1, Stage 1*
Sterilise all equipment as required. See *Apple 1, Stage 2*
Start records

Wash and crush the blackcurrants; wash the dried currants and sultanas and lightly liquidise just enough to break the skin. Place in a white plastic bucket with 2.5 litres (4½ pints) of water, 1 crushed Campden tablet or 5 ml (1 tsp) of strong sulphite solution, the pectin-destroying enzyme, yeast nutrient and vitamin B₁ tablet. Boil the peeled, sliced bananas in 1 litre (1¾ pints) of water for 20 minutes; strain and add to the other ingredients. Leave for 24 hours before adding the yeast starter. Ferment on the pulp for four days, breaking up the fruit cap two or three times daily, before straining the liquid, pressing the pulp lightly. Add the sugar and pour into the demijohn. Proceed as in **Apple 1, Stage 4**.

Mature in bulk for 6 months before bottling and in bottle for another 12 months.

CHERRY 1
(cold water infusion, freezing)

1.5 kg (3$\frac{1}{3}$ lb) morello or early river cherries
426 ml ($\frac{3}{4}$ pint) red grape concentrate
600 g (1$\frac{1}{2}$ lb) sugar
Water to 4.5 litres (1 gal.)

5 g (1 tsp) pectin-destroying enzyme
5 g (1 tsp) yeast nutrient
1 vitamin B$_1$ tablet
Bordeaux type yeast
Campden tablets or strong sulphite solution

De-stalk and wash the cherries and place in the freezer for 24 hours

Activate the yeast starter bottle. See *Apple 1, Stage 1*
Sterilise all equipment as required. See *Apple 1, Stage 2*
Start records

Remove the cherries from the freezer and place in a white plastic bucket; pour 2 litres (3$\frac{1}{2}$ pints) of near boiling water over the fruit. As the water cools, the cherries can be squashed by hand. Add 1 crushed Campden tablet or 5 ml (1 tsp) of strong sulphite solution, the pectin-destroying enzyme, yeast nutrient and vitamin B$_1$ tablet. Stir well and cover with an upturned plate to ensure the fruits are covered by liquid. Replace lid. Stir the must two or three times daily for three days to ensure a good extraction from the fruit. Strain off the liquid, pressing the pulp lightly, and add the grape concentrate and stir. A hydrometer reading can be taken at this stage (see **Apple 2, Stage 1**). Dissolve the sugar in 1 litre (1$\frac{3}{4}$ pints) of water and add to the must with the active yeast starter. Pour into the demijohn and fit an airlock. Proceed as in **Apple 1, Stage 4**.

Mature in bulk for 6 months before bottling.

CHERRY 2
(pulp fermentation)

1 kg jar Karkus morello or fresh cherries
453 g (1 lb) sloes or bullaces
453 g (1 lb) white sultanas
700 g (1$\frac{1}{2}$ lb) sugar
Water to 4.5 litres (1 gal.)

5 g (1 tsp) pectin-destroying enzyme
5 g (1 tsp) yeast nutrient
1 vitamin B$_1$ tablet
Bordeaux type yeast
Campden tablets or strong sulphite solution

Activate the yeast starter bottle. See *Apple 1, Stage 1*
Sterilise all equipment as required. See *Apple 1, Stage 2*
Start records

Wash and crush the sloes and cherries, taking care not to break the stones. Chop or lightly liquidise the sultanas and place in the white plastic bucket, adding 2.5 litres (4$\frac{1}{2}$ pints) of cold water, 1 crushed Campden tablet or 5ml (1 tsp) of strong sulphite solution, the pectin-destroying enzyme, yeast nutrient and vitamin B$_1$ tablet. Stir well, replace lid and leave for 24 hours before

adding the active yeast starter. Ferment on the pulp for three days, keeping the fruit submerged with an upturned plate and the lid of the bucket tightly fitted. Stir the pulp two or three times daily to break up the fruit cap. Strain into another bucket, pressing the pulp lightly. Add the sugar and when fully dissolved pour into the demijohn. Proceed as in **Apple 1, Stage 4**.

Mature in bulk for 6 months before bottling.

CHERRY AND GRAPE
(pulp fermentation)

1.5 kg (3¹/₃ lb) morello or early river cherries	5 g (1 tsp) pectin-destroying enzyme
3 kg (6 lb 10 oz) black grapes	5 g (1 tsp) yeast nutrient
600 g (1¹/₃ lb) sugar	1 vitamin B1 tablet
Water to 4.5 litres (1 gal.)	Burgundy or Bordeaux type yeast
	Campden tablets or strong sulphite solution

Activate the yeast starter bottle. See *Apple 1, Stage 1*
Sterilise all equipment as required. See *Apple 1, Stage 2*
Start records

Wash and crush the cherries and grapes and place in a white plastic bucket. Add 1.25 litres (2¹/₄ pints) of water, 1 crushed Campden tablet or 5 ml (1 tsp) of strong sulphite solution, the pectin-destroying enzyme, yeast nutrient and vitamin B₁ tablet. Stir well and keep the fruit submerged with an upturned plate placed on top of the fruit. Replace lid and leave for 24 hours. Add the active yeast starter and ferment on the pulp for five days, breaking up the fruit cap two or three times daily. Strain. Dissolve the sugar in the must and pour into the demijohn. Proceed as in **Apple 1, Stage 4**.

Mature in bulk for 6 months before bottling and in bottle for 12 months. This wine is rather expensive to make, so the cherries should be purchased and frozen until cheaper grapes arrive in the autumn. Alternatively, use two jars of bottled cherries, but the wine will lack a little vitality.

DAMSON
(cold water infusion, freezing)

1.5 kg (3¹/₃ lb) damsons	5 g (1 tsp) pectin-destroying enzyme
453 g (1 lb) dried currants	5 g (1 tsp) yeast nutrient
3 ripe bananas	1 vitamin B₁ tablet
800 g (1³/₄ lb) sugar	Burgundy type yeast
Water to 4.5 litres (1 gal.)	Campden tablets or strong sulphite solution

Wash the damsons and place in the freezer for 48 hours.

Activate the yeast starter bottle. See *Apple 1, Stage 1*
Sterilise all equipment as required. See *Apple 1, Stage 2*
Start records

Remove the damsons from the freezer and place in a white plastic bucket with the washed and lightly liquidised (just breaking the skins) dried currants. Pour 2 litres (3½ pints) of near boiling water over the fruit and as the water cools, the damsons will be able to be crushed by hand. Add 1 crushed Campden tablet or 5 ml (1 tsp) of strong sulphite solution, the pectin-destroying enzyme, yeast nutrient and vitamin B_1 tablet. Skin the bananas, slice and boil in 500 ml (18 fl oz) of water for 20 minutes. Strain the liquid into the fruit. Stir well and cover with an upturned plate to keep the fruit submerged. Replace lid. Leave for three days, stirring the fruit pulp two or three times daily to break up the fruit cap. Strain and pour the must into a demijohn for the sediment to drop out. Siphon the clear liquid from the sediment into a bucket.

A hydrometer reading can be taken at this stage (see **Apple 2, Stage 1**). Dissolve the sugar in 1 litre (1¾ pints) of water and add to the must with the yeast starter. Pour into the demijohn and fit an airlock. Proceed as in **Apple 1, Stage 4**.

Mature in bulk for three months before bottling and in bottle for 12 months.

ELDERBERRY 1
(pulp fermentation)

1 kg (2¼ lb) elderberries	5 g (1 tsp) pectin-destroying enzyme
500 g (1lb 1½ oz) sloes, bullaces or damsons	5 g (1 tsp) yeast nutrient
	1 vitamin B_1 tablet
500 g (1lb 1½ oz) dried currants	Burgundy or Bordeaux type
500 g (1lb 1½ oz) sultanas	yeast
900 g (2 lb) sugar	Campden tablets or strong
Water to 4.5 litres (1 gal.)	sulphite solution

Activate the yeast starter bottle. See *Apple 1, Stage 1*
Sterilise all equipment as required. See *Apple 1, Stage 2*
Start records

Strip the elderberries from the stems and wash them, removing any green ones that float to the surface. Crush the berries with the sloes, wash the currants and sultanas and lightly liquidise (only just breaking the skins) and place in a plastic bucket with 3 litres (5¼ pints) of cold water, 1 crushed Campden tablet or 5 ml (1 tsp) of strong sulphite solution, the pectin-destroying enzyme, yeast nutrient and vitamin B_1 tablet. Stir well and leave for 24 hours before adding the active yeast starter. Proceed as in **Apple 1, Stage 3** before adding the sugar. Proceed to **Apple 1, Stage 4**.

Mature in bulk for 6 months before bottling. Store the wine in bottle for another 12 months.

ELDERBERRY 2
(pasteurised)

1 kg (2¼ lb) elderberries
500 g (1lb 1½ oz) blackberries
3 ripe bananas
1 litre (1¾ pints) of red grape juice
800 g (1¾ lb) sugar
10 g (2 tsp) tartaric acid
Water to 4.5 litres (1 gal.)

5 g (1 tsp) pectin-destroying enzyme
5 g (1 tsp) yeast nutrient
1 vitamin B_1 tablet
Burgundy or Bordeaux type yeast
Campden tablets or strong sulphite
solution

Activate the yeast starter bottle. See *Apple 1, Stage 1*
Sterilise all equipment as required. See *Apple 1, Stage 2*
Start records

Wash the elderberries and blackberries and place in a large stainless steel saucepan with 1.5 litres (2¾ pints) of water. Heat to a temperature of 65 °C (150 °F), maintaining the temperature for 5 minutes. Pour into a white plastic bucket. Boil the peeled, sliced bananas in 500 ml (18 fl oz) of water for 20 minutes. Strain the liquid into the elderberries and blackberry must and when cool add the grape juice, pectin-destroying enzyme, yeast nutrient, tartaric acid and vitamin B_1 tablet. Stir well. Replace lid. After 24 hours strain off the liquid, pressing the pulp. Add the active yeast starter and pour into the demijohn. Plug the top with cotton wool; this will enable the fermentation to become active within 24 hours, and then fit an airlock. Dissolve the sugar in 1 litre (1¾ pints) of water and add to the demijohn. Proceed as in **Apple 1, Stage 4.**

Mature in bulk for 6 months before bottling.

ELDERBERRY 3
(pulp fermentation, freezing)

1 kg (2¼ lb) elderberries
3 kg (6 lb 10 oz) black grapes
453 g (1 lb) sultanas
5 g (1 tsp) tartaric acid
800 g (1¾ lb) sugar
Water to 4.5 litres (1 gal.)

5 g (1 tsp) pectin-destroying enzyme
5 g (1 tsp) yeast nutrient
1 vitamin B_1 tablet
Burgundy or Bordeaux type yeast
Campden tablets or strong sulphite
solution

Wash the elderberries and grapes, remove the stalks and place in a plastic bag and put in the freezer for 24 hours.

Activate the yeast starter bottle. See *Apple 1, Stage 1*
Sterilise all equipment as required. See *Apple 1, Stage 2*
Start records

Remove the elderberries and grapes from the freezer and place in a white plastic bucket. As the fruit thaws it can easily be crushed by hand or squashed with a litre bottle. Wash and chop or lightly liquidise the sultanas in order to break the skins. Add to the bucket with 1 Campden tablet or 5 ml (1 tsp) strong sulphite solution, tartaric acid, pectin-destroying enzyme, yeast nutrient, vitamin B_1 tablet and 2 litres ($3^{1}/_2$ pints) of water. Stir well and cover with an upturned dinner plate to keep the fruit submerged. Replace lid. Leave for 24 hours before adding the active yeast starter. Proceed as in **Apple 1, Stage 3** before adding the sugar. Proceed as in **Apple 1, Stage 4**.

Mature in bulk for 6 months before bottling and 12 months in bottle.

GOOSEBERRY 1
(cold water infusion, freezing)

1.5 kg ($3^{1}/_3$ lb) gooseberries	5 g (1 tsp) pectin-destroying enzyme
1 kg ($2^{1}/_4$ lb) pears	5 g (1 tsp) yeast nutrient
453 g (1lb) sultanas	1 vitamin B_1 tablet
800 g ($1^{3}/_4$ lb) sugar	Hock or Chablis type yeast
5 g (1 tsp) tartaric acid	Campden tablets or strong sulphite
Water to 4.5 litres (1 gal.)	solution

Wash the gooseberries and pears and place in the freezer for 48 hours.

Activate the yeast starter bottle. See *Apple 1, Stage 1*
Sterilise all equipment as required. See *Apple 1, Stage 2*
Start records

Remove the gooseberries and pears from the freezer and place in a white plastic bucket; pour 2.5 litres ($4^{1}/_2$ pints) of near boiling water over the fruit. As the water cools, the fruit can be squashed by hand. Wash the sultanas and chop and add to the fruit with 1 crushed Campden tablet or 5 ml (1 tsp) of strong sulphite solution, the pectin-destroying enzyme, yeast nutrient, tartaric acid and vitamin B_1 tablet. Stir well, cover with an upturned dinner plate to ensure the fruit is covered by liquid. Replace lid. Leave for two days, stirring two or three times daily to enable a good extraction rate from the fruits. Strain off the liquid into another bucket, pressing the pulp. A hydrometer reading can be taken at this stage (see **Apple 2, Stage 1**). Dissolve the sugar in the must, add the active yeast and pour into the demijohn. Proceed as in **Apple 1, Stage 4**.

Mature in bulk for 6 months before bottling.

GOOSEBERRY 2

(pulp fermentation)

1 kg (2¼ lb) gooseberries	5 g (1 tsp) pectin-destroying enzyme
200 g (7 oz) of 'ready to eat' dried apricots	5 g (1 tsp) yeast nutrient
	1 vitamin B₁ tablet
453 g (1 lb) white sultanas	Chablis or White Chardonnay type yeast
600 g (1⅓ lb) sugar	Campden tablets or strong sulphite
Water to 4.5 litres (1 gal.)	solution

Activate the yeast starter bottle. See *Apple 1, Stage 1*
Sterilise all equipment as required. See *Apple 1, Stage 2*
Start records

Crush the gooseberries, wash and chop the apricots and sultanas and place in a white plastic bucket. Add 2.5 litres (4½ pints) of cold water, 1 crushed Campden tablet or 5 ml (1 tsp) of strong sulphite solution, the pectin-destroying enzyme, yeast nutrient and vitamin B₁ tablet. Stir well and leave for 24 hours before adding the active yeast starter. Proceed as in **Apple 1, Stage 3** before adding the sugar. Proceed as in **Apple 1, Stage 4.**

Mature in bulk for 3 months before bottling. The wine will improve if stored for another 12 months.

GOOSEBERRY 3

(cold water infusion, freezing)

1.5 kg (3⅓ lb) gooseberries	5 g (1 tsp) pectin-destroying enzyme
1 kg (2¼ lb) pears	5 g (1 tsp) yeast nutrient
1 litre (1¾ pints) grape juice	1 vitamin B₁ tablet
700 g (1½ lb) sugar	Chablis or White Chardonnay type yeast
Water to 4.5 litres (1 gal.)	Campden tablet or strong sulphite solution

Wash the gooseberries and pears and place in the freezer for 24 hours.

Activate the yeast starter bottle. See *Apple 1, Stage 1*
Sterilise all equipment as required. See *Apple 1, Stage 2*
Start records

Remove the fruit from the freezer and place in a white plastic bucket. Pour 2 litres (3½ pints) of near boiling water over the fruit. As the fruit thaws they can easily be squashed by hand. Add 1 crushed Campden tablet, the pectin-destroying enzyme, yeast nutrient and vitamin B₁ tablet. Stir well and cover with an upturned dinner plate. Replace lid. Leave for three days, stirring the must two or three times daily. Strain off the liquid into another bucket, pressing the pulp, and stir in the sugar and grape juice. A more delicate wine will be achieved if left for 12 hours before siphoning off the clear liquid into a demijohn. Add the active yeast starter and plug the top of the jar with cotton wool to help the fermentation start quickly. After 24 hours replace with an airlock. Proceed as in **Apple 1, Stage 4**. Mature in bulk for 6 months before bottling.

GOOSEBERRY 4
(pulp fermentation)

1.5 kg (3¹/₃ lb) gooseberries
4 ripe bananas
1 litre (1³/₄ pints) of orchard
fresh apple juice
700 g (1¹/₂ lb) sugar
15 to 20 white rose petals
Water to 4.5 litres (1 gal.)

5 g (1 tsp) pectin-destroying enzyme
5 g (1 tsp) yeast nutrient
1 vitamin B₁ tablet
Chardonnay or Chablis type yeast
Campden tablets or strong sulphite
solution

Activate the yeast starter bottle. See *Apple 1, Stage 1*
Sterilise all equipment as required. See *Apple 1, Stage 2*
Start records

Wash the gooseberries and cut or crush them before placing in a white plastic bucket with 1.5 litres (2³/₄ pints) of water. Boil the peeled sliced bananas in 1 litre (1³/₄ pints) of water for 20 minutes, then strain off the liquid into the gooseberries. Add 1 crushed Campden tablet or 5 ml (1 tsp) of strong sulphite solution, the pectin-destroying enzyme, yeast nutrient, vitamin B₁ tablet, fresh apple juice and the crushed rose petals. Stir well and cover with an upturned dinner plate to keep the fruit submerged. Replace lid. After 24 hours add the active yeast starter and ferment on the pulp for 48 hours. Stir two or three times daily in order to break up the fruit cap before straining off the liquid into another bucket, pressing the pulp. Add the sugar and when dissolved pour into the demijohn. Proceed as in **Apple 1, Stage 4**.

Mature in bulk for 6 months before bottling.

LOGANBERRY
(cold water infusion, freezing)

1 kg (2¹/₄ lb) loganberries
1 kg (2¹/₄ lb) pears
2 litres (3¹/₂ pints) red grape juice
600 g (1¹/₃ lb) sugar
Water to 4.5 litres (1 gal.)

5 g (1 tsp) pectin-destroying enzyme
5 g (1 tsp) yeast nutrient
1 vitamin B₁ tablet
Bordeaux type yeast
Campden tablets or strong sulphite
solution

Wash the loganberries and pears and place in the freezer for 48 hours.

Activate the yeast starter bottle. See *Apple 1, Stage 1*
Sterilise all equipment as required. See *Apple 1, Stage 2*
Start records

Remove the loganberries and pears from the freezer and place in a
white plastic bucket. Pour over 1.5 litres (2³/₄ pints) of near boiling
water. As the fruit thaws it can easily be crushed by hand. Add the red
grape juice, 1 crushed Campden tablet or 5 ml (1 tsp) of strong sulphite
solution, the pectin-destroying enzyme, yeast nutrient and vitamin B_1 tablet.
Stir well and cover with an upturned dinner plate to keep the fruit
submerged. Replace lid. Stir the must two or three times daily
for three days to ensure a good extraction from the fruit.
Strain off the liquid into another bucket, pressing the pulp
lightly, add the sugar and the active yeast starter. Pour
into a demijohn and plug the top of the jar with cotton
wool to help the fermentation start quickly. After 24
hours replace with an airlock. Proceed as in **Apple 1, Stage 4**.

Mature in bulk for 6 months before bottling. Store in bottle for
another 6 months.

PEAR AND PINEAPPLE
(pulp fermentation, freezing)

1.5 kg (3¹/₃ lb) pears
1 large ripe fresh pineapple
1 litre (1³/₄ pints) white grape juice
5 g (1 tsp) tartaric acid
700 g (1¹/₂ lb) sugar
Water to 4.5 litres (1 gal.)

5 g (1 tsp) pectin-destroying
enzyme
5 g (1 tsp) yeast nutrient
1 vitamin B_1 tablet
Hock type yeast
Campden tablets or strong
sulphite solution

Peel the pineapple, removing the inner core and slice into cubes. Wash the pears
and place with the pineapple in a plastic bag into the freezer for 48 hours.

Activate the yeast starter bottle. See *Apple 1, Stage 1*
Sterilise all equipment as required. See *Apple 1, Stage 2*
Start records

Remove the fruit from the freezer and place in a white plastic bucket. Pour 2
litres (3¹/₂ pints) of near boiling water over the fruit. As it thaws the pears
and pineapple will easily be crushed by hand. Add 1 Campden tablet, tartaric
acid, pectin-destroying enzyme, yeast nutrient and vitamin B_1 tablet. Stir well
and cover with an upturned dinner plate to keep the fruit submerged.
Replace lid. Leave for 24 hours. Add the white grape juice and active yeast
starter. Proceed as in **Apple 1, Stage 3** before adding the sugar.

Proceed as in **Apple 1, Stage 4**. Mature in bulk for 6 months before
bottling.

PEAR AND GREEN PLUMS
(pulp fermentation)

1 kg (2¹/₄ lb) cooking pears
1 kg (2¹/₄ lb) greengages
453 g (1lb) sultanas
5 g (1 tsp) tartaric acid
720 g (1lb 9¹/₂ oz) sugar
Water to 4.5 litres (1 gal.)

5 g (1 tsp) pectin-destroying enzyme
5 g (1 tsp) yeast nutrient
1 vitamin B₁ tablet
White Bordeaux or Hock type yeast
Campden tablets or strong sulphite
solution

Activate the yeast starter bottle. See *Apple 1, Stage 1*
Sterilise all equipment as required. See *Apple 1, Stage 2*
Start records

Wash the pears and greengages. Put 1 crushed Campden tablet or 5 ml (1 tsp) of strong sulphite solution in 2.5 litres (4¹/₂ pints) of water into a bucket. Slice the pears directly into the bucket to prevent oxidation. Stone the greengages, quarter them and add to the pears. Wash the sultanas, chop and add with the tartaric acid, pectin-destroying enzyme, yeast nutrient and vitamin B₁ tablet. Stir well and cover with an upturned dinner plate to keep the fruit submerged. Replace lid. After 24 hours add the active yeast starter. Proceed as in **Apple 1, Stage 3** before adding the sugar. Proceed as in **Apple 1, Stage 4.**

   Mature in bulk for 6 months and in bottle for a further 6 months.

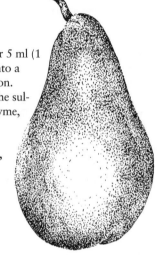

PINEAPPLE
(pulp fermentation)

1 large fresh pineapple
600 g (1¹/₃ lb) white sultanas
3 ripe bananas
5 g (1 tsp) tartaric acid
780 g (1 lb 11¹/₂ oz) sugar
Water to 4.5 litres (1 gal.)

5 g (1 tsp) pectin-destroying enzyme
5 g (1 tsp) yeast nutrient
1 vitamin B₁ tablet
Chablis type yeast
Campden tablets or strong sulphite
solution

Activate the yeast starter bottle. See *Apple 1, Stage 1*
Sterilise all equipment as required. See *Apple 1, Stage 2*
Start records

Select a fully ripened pineapple. Peel and remove the hard core. Slice into small pieces and put in a bucket. Add 2.5 litres (4¹/₂ pints) of cold water and 1 crushed Campden tablet or 5 ml (1 tsp) strong sulphite solution. Slice the peeled bananas and boil for 20 minutes, strain off the liquid into the pineapple. Wash the sultanas and chop or very lightly liquidise, just enough to break some of the skins, and add to the must with the pectin-destroying enzyme, yeast nutrient and vitamin B₁ tablet. Stir well and cover with an upturned dinner plate. Leave for 24 hours before adding the active yeast starter. Proceed as in **Apple 1, Stage 3** before adding the sugar. Proceed as in **Apple 1, Stage 4.**
   Mature in bulk for 3 months and in bottle for another 6 months.

RASPBERRY

(pasteurised)

500 g (1lb 1^1/$_2$ oz) raspberries	5 g (1 tsp) pectin-destroying enzyme
453 g (1 lb) redcurrants	5 g (1 tsp) yeast nutrient
426 ml (^{1}/$_2$ pint) red grape concentrate	1 vitamin B$_1$ tablet
600 g (1^1/$_3$ lb) sugar	Bordeaux type yeast
Water to 4.5 litres (1 gal.)	Campden tablets or strong sulphite solution

Activate the yeast starter bottle. See *Apple 1, Stage 1*
Sterilise all equipment as required. See *Apple 1, Stage 2*
Start records

Wash and de-stalk the redcurrants and place in a large stainless steel saucepan
with 1.5 litres (2^3/$_4$ pints) of water. Heat to a temperature of 65 °C (150 °F),
maintaining the heat for 5 minutes. Remove from the heat and add the
raspberries. Pour into a bucket, adding the grape concentrate. Cool slightly
before adding 1 crushed Campden tablet or 5 ml (1 tsp) of strong sulphite
solution, the pectin-destroying enzyme, yeast nutrient and vitamin B$_1$
tablet. Stir well, replace the lid on the bucket and leave for 48 hours,
stirring two or three times daily, before straining into another bucket
and pressing the pulp. A hydrometer reading can be taken at this stage
(see **Apple 2, Stage 1**). Dissolve the sugar in 1 litre (1^3/$_4$ pints) of water,
stirring until dissolved, and add to the strained must with the active yeast
starter. Pour into a demijohn and fit an airlock. Proceed as in **Apple 1, Stage 4**.
   Mature in bulk for 6 months and in bottle for another 6 months.

ROSEHIP

(pulp fermentation)

1 kg (2^1/$_4$ lb) rosehips	5 g (1 tsp) pectin-destroying enzyme
1 kg (2^1/$_4$ lb) dessert apples	5 g (1 tsp) yeast nutrient
1 litre (1^3/$_4$ pints) white grape juice	1 vitamin B$_1$ tablet
453 g (1lb) white sultanas	Chablis or Hock type yeast
700 g (1^1/$_2$ lb) sugar	Campden tablets or strong sulphite solution
Water to 4.5 litres (1 gal.)	

Activate the yeast starter bottle. See *Apple 1, Stage 1*
Sterilise all equipment as required. See *Apple 1, Stage 2*
Start records

After washing, crush the rosehips, cut the apples in small cubes and place in a
bucket with 1 crushed Campden tablet or 5 ml (1 tsp) of strong sulphite solution and 2.5 litres (4^1/$_2$ pints) of water. Wash the sultanas and chop and add
to the fruit with the white grape juice, the pectin-destroying enzyme, yeast
nutrient and vitamin B$_1$ tablet. Stir well and keep the fruit submerged with an
upturned dinner plate. Replace lid and leave for 24 hours. Add the active yeast
starter and proceed as in **Apple 1, Stage 3** before adding the sugar. Proceed as
in **Apple 1, Stage 4**. Mature in bulk for 6 months before bottling.

SLOE 1
(pasteurised, pulp fermentation)

1 kg (2¹/₄ lb) sloes
1 kg (2¹/₄ lb) cooking pears
453 g (1lb) raisins
900 g (2 lb) sugar
Water to 4.5 litres (1 gal.)

5 g (1 tsp) pectin-destroying enzyme
5 g (1 tsp) yeast nutrient
1 vitamin B₁ tablet
French style yeast
Campden tablets or strong sulphite
solution

Activate the yeast starter bottle. See *Apple 1, Stage 1*
Sterilise all equipment as required. See *Apple 1, Stage 2*
Start records

Wash the sloes and pears. Crush the sloes and quarter the pears and place in a stainless steel saucepan with 2 litres (3¹/₂ pints) of water. Heat to 65 °C (150 °F), maintaining the heat for 5 minutes. Pour into a bucket. Wash the raisins and chop, adding them to the fruit. Cool slightly before adding the pectin-destroying enzyme, yeast nutrient and vitamin B₁ tablet. Stir well, replace lid and leave for 24 hours. It is not necessary to add any sulphite solution at this stage, as the fruits have been pasteurised. Add the active yeast starter and proceed as in **Apple 1, Stage 3** before adding the sugar. Proceed as in **Apple 1, Stage 4**.

Mature in bulk for 12 months before bottling. Store for a further 6 months.

SLOE 2
(cold water infusion, freezing)

1 kg (2¹/₄ lb) sloes or bullaces
1 kg (2¹/₄ lb) dessert pears
426 ml (³/₄ pint) red grape concentrate
700 g (1¹/₂ lb) sugar
Water to 4.5 litres (1 gal.)

5 g (1 tsp) pectin-destroying enzyme
5 g (1 tsp) yeast nutrient
1 vitamin B₁ tablet
French style yeast
Campden tablets or strong sulphite
solution

Wash the sloes or bullaces and pears and put in a plastic bag and place in the freezer for 48 hours.

Activate the yeast starter bottle. See *Apple 1, Stage 1*
Sterilise all equipment as required. See *Apple 1, Stage 2*
Start records

Remove the sloes or bullaces and pears from the freezer and place in a white plastic bucket. Pour over 1.75 litres (3 pints) of near boiling water and as the fruits thaw they can be crushed by hand. Add 1 crushed Campden tablet or 5 ml (1 tsp) of strong sulphite solution, the pectin-destroying enzyme, yeast nutrient and vitamin B₁ tablet. Stir well and cover with an upturned plate to keep the fruits submerged. Replace lid. Leave the fruit for three days, stirring two or three times daily to distribute the fruit pulp. After three days strain off the liquid into another bucket, pressing the pulp lightly, and stir in the grape concentrate. A hydrometer reading can be taken at this stage (see **Apple 2, Stage 1**). Dissolve the sugar in 1 litre (1¾ pints) of water and add to the must. Pour into a demijohn and add the active yeast starter. Plug the top with cotton wool to enable the fermentation to become established. After 24 hours replace with an airlock. Proceed as in **Apple 1, Stage 4**.

Mature in bulk for 6 months before bottling. Store for a further 6 months.

STRAWBERRY
(cold water infusion)

1 kg (2¼ lb) strawberries	5 g (1 tsp) pectin-destroying enzyme
340 g (¾ lb) gooseberries	5 g (1 tsp) yeast nutrient
1 litre (1¾ pints) apple juice	1 vitamin B₁ tablet
5 g (1 tsp) tartaric acid	Bordeaux type yeast
650 g (1 lb 7 oz) sugar	Campden tablets or strong sulphite
Water to 4.5 litres (1 gal.)	solution

Activate the yeast starter bottle. See *Apple 1, Stage 1*
Sterilise all equipment as required. See *Apple 1, Stage 2*
Start records

De-stalk and wash the strawberries and gooseberries and crush in a white plastic bucket, add 1 litre (1¾ pints) of water and 1 litre (1¾ pints) of apple juice, 1 crushed Campden tablet or 5 ml (1 tsp) of strong sulphite solution, the pectin-destroying enzyme, tartaric acid, yeast nutrient and vitamin B₁ tablet. Stir well and place an upturned dinner plate on top of the fruit to keep it submerged. Replace lid. Leave for three days, stirring the fruit two or three times daily. Strain with a fine muslin or nylon cloth into a bucket. A hydrometer reading can be taken at this stage (see **Apple 2, Stage 1**). Dissolve the sugar in 1 litre (1¾ pints) of cold water and add to the must. Pour into the demijohn and add the yeast starter. Plug the top with cotton wool to enable the fermentation to become established. After 24 hours replace with an airlock. Proceed as in **Apple 1, Stage 4**.

Mature in bulk for 3 months before bottling.

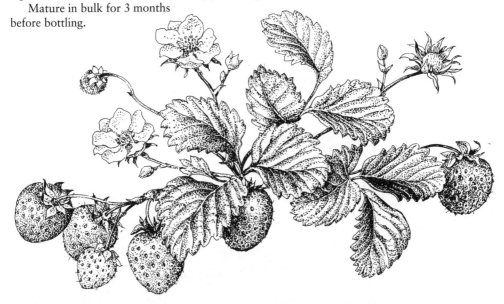

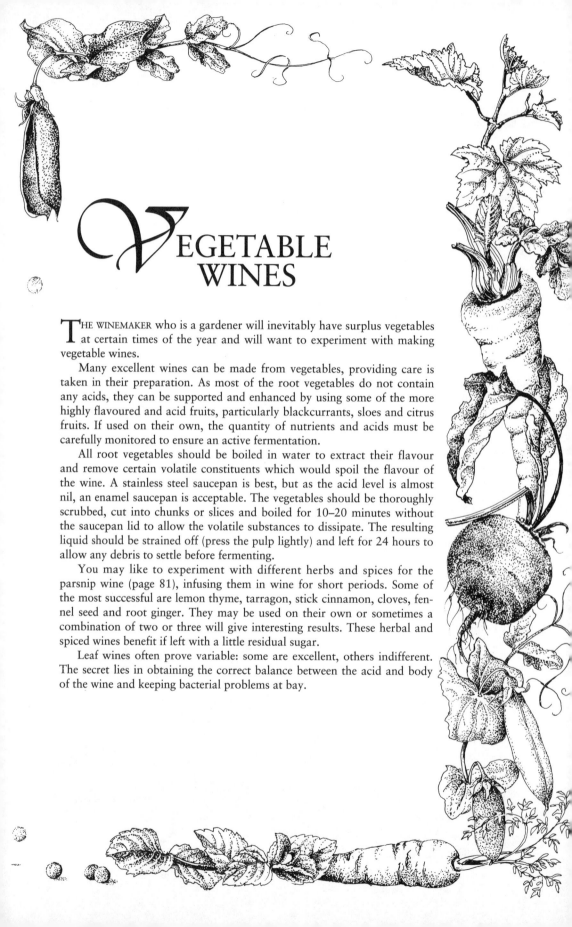

VEGETABLE WINES

THE WINEMAKER who is a gardener will inevitably have surplus vegetables at certain times of the year and will want to experiment with making vegetable wines.

Many excellent wines can be made from vegetables, providing care is taken in their preparation. As most of the root vegetables do not contain any acids, they can be supported and enhanced by using some of the more highly flavoured and acid fruits, particularly blackcurrants, sloes and citrus fruits. If used on their own, the quantity of nutrients and acids must be carefully monitored to ensure an active fermentation.

All root vegetables should be boiled in water to extract their flavour and remove certain volatile constituents which would spoil the flavour of the wine. A stainless steel saucepan is best, but as the acid level is almost nil, an enamel saucepan is acceptable. The vegetables should be thoroughly scrubbed, cut into chunks or slices and boiled for 10–20 minutes without the saucepan lid to allow the volatile substances to dissipate. The resulting liquid should be strained off (press the pulp lightly) and left for 24 hours to allow any debris to settle before fermenting.

You may like to experiment with different herbs and spices for the parsnip wine (page 81), infusing them in wine for short periods. Some of the most successful are lemon thyme, tarragon, stick cinnamon, cloves, fennel seed and root ginger. They may be used on their own or sometimes a combination of two or three will give interesting results. These herbal and spiced wines benefit if left with a little residual sugar.

Leaf wines often prove variable: some are excellent, others indifferent. The secret lies in obtaining the correct balance between the acid and body of the wine and keeping bacterial problems at bay.

BEETROOT 1

Sulphite for sterilising: Dissolve 8 Campden tablets or 14 g sodium or potassium metabisulphite in 1 litre (1¾ pints) of water and store in a screw-topped bottle.

Strong sulphite solution: Add 28 g (1 oz) sodium or potassium metabisulphite to 500 ml (18 fl oz) of water. Store in a screw-topped bottle.

Yeast starter bottle: Sterilise a small bottle either by boiling for 5 minutes or filling with sterilising sulphite and leaving for 20 minutes. Pour back into the storage bottle and rinse twice to remove any sulphite solution. Half fill the bottle with cooled boiled water, add the juice from half a lemon (approx. 25 ml), 10 g (2 tsp) of granulated sugar and the wine yeast. Shake the bottle, plug with cotton wool and leave in a warm place, 18–21 °C (65–70 °F), for 48 hours.

2 kg (4½ lb) beetroot	5 g (1 tsp) pectin-destroying enzyme
453 g (1 lb) blackcurrants or	5 g (1 tsp) yeast nutrient
226 g (½ lb) each of sloes	1 vitamin B_1 tablet
and blackberries	Burgundy type yeast
226 g (½ lb) currants	Campden tablets or strong sulphite
226 g (½ lb) sultanas	solution
5 g (1 tsp) malic acid	
906 g (2 lb) sugar	
Water to 4.5 litres (1 gal.)	

Activate the yeast starter bottle
Start records

Sterilise all equipment as required. Prepare the covered plastic bucket and utensils by washing thoroughly with warm water. Place the utensils to be used in the bucket: pour in the sterilising solution. Replace lid tightly and swirl the solution around, making sure that it reaches all part of the bucket. Leave for 20 minutes (longer if possible) before returning the solution to the storage bottle. It will remain effective for quite a long while, providing it retains its pungent odour. Carefully wash the bucket and utensils with tap water to remove all traces of sulphite before use.

Wash the blackcurrants (or blackberries and sloes), the dried currants and sultanas, lightly liquidise or crush them and place in a fermentation bucket with 1 litre (1¾ pints) of cold water. Add 1 crushed Campden tablet or 5 ml (1 tsp) of strong sulphite solution, the malic acid, pectin-destroying enzyme, yeast nutrient and vitamin B_1 tablet and cover.

    Wash and scrub the beetroots and slice them; cover with 1.5 litres (2¾ pints) of cold water and bring to the boil. Boil for 30 minutes without the lid. Strain the liquid from the pulp and leave to settle. After 24 hours siphon the clear liquid from the sediment into the other ingredients in the bucket. Stir and add the active yeast starter, pouring it carefully into the fruit pulp at one side to enable a colony to become established. Cover the bucket tightly. When the yeast activity is obvious, stir it into the bulk and ferment on the pulp for three days, keeping the fruit submerged with an upturned dinner plate. Strain and add the sugar before pouring into the demijohn.

* The jar should be no more than seven-eighths full. Fit an airlock and leave in a warm place, 18–21 °C (65–70 °F), to ferment. Top up after a few days with a little cold water. When the fermentation ceases it is advisable to add a fining agent in order for the wine to clear quickly; use either bentonite or a simple and effective wine clearing kit (see pages 25–27 on Clearing) and move to a cooler place. After three days siphon the clearing wine into a clean demijohn, adding 2 crushed Campden tablets or 10 ml (2 tsp) of strong sulphite solution. Top up with a little cold water. Rack again after two weeks, adding 2 more Campden tablets or 10 ml (2 tsp) of strong sulphite solution. Top up with water and replace airlock with a bung. Store in a cool place. If a deposit forms, rack again, but it will not be necessary to add any more sulphite.

Mature in bulk for 12 months before bottling.

BEETROOT 2

2 kg (4¹/₂ lb) beetroot
426 ml (³/₄ pint) red grape juice
15 g (2 tbsp) tartaric acid
5 g (1 tsp) malic acid
2 g grape tannin
900 g (2 lb) sugar
Water to 4.5 litres (1 gal.)

5 g (1 tsp) pectin-destroying enzyme
5 g (1 tsp) yeast nutrient
2 vitamin B₁ tablets
Burgundy type yeast
Campden tablets or
strong sulphite solution

Activate the yeast starter bottle. See *Beetroot 1*
Sterilise all equipment as required. See *Beetroot 1*
Start records

Wash and scrub the beetroots, slice them and cover with 3 litres (5¹/₄ pints) of cold water; bring to the boil. Boil for 30 minutes without the lid. Strain from the pulp and leave to settle. After 24 hours siphon the clear liquid from the sediment, add the red grape juice, tartaric and malic acids, grape tannin, pectin-destroying enzyme, yeast nutrient and vitamin B₁ tablet. Stir until the ingredients are dissolved and pour into a demijohn, adding the active yeast starter. Plug the top with cotton wool. When the fermentation is active dissolve the sugar in the fermenting must and fit an airlock. Proceed as * in Beetroot 1.

Mature in bulk for 12 months before bottling.

CARROT 1

1.5 kg (3¹/₃ lb) carrots
4 small bananas
Juice from 4 oranges
50 ml (2 fl oz) lemon juice
10 g (2 tsp) tartaric acid
2 g grape tannin
900 g (2 lb) sugar
Water to 4.5 litres (1 gal.)

5 g (1 tsp) pectin-destroying enzyme
5 g (1 tsp) yeast nutrient
1 vitamin B_1 tablet
Bordeaux type yeast
Campden tablets or strong sulphite
solution

Activate the yeast starter bottle. See *Beetroot 1*
Sterilise all equipment as required. See *Beetroot 1*
Start records

Wash and scrub the carrots, slice them thinly and place in a
saucepan with 2.5 litres (4¹/₂ pints) of cold water. Skin the
bananas, slice finely and add with a little grated peel from 2
oranges. Boil for 30 minutes without the lid. Strain from the
pulp and leave to settle. After 24 hours siphon the clear liquid
from the sediment, add the orange and lemon juice, tartaric acid,
grape tannin, pectin-destroying enzyme, yeast nutrient and vitamin B_1
tablet. Stir well until the ingredients are dissolved and pour into the demijohn, adding the active yeast starter. Plug the top with cotton wool. When
the fermentation is active dissolve the sugar in 1 litre (1³/₄ pints) of water
and add to the demijohn. Fit an airlock. Proceed as * in **Beetroot 1**.
  Mature in bulk for 15 months before bottling.

CARROT 2

1.5 kg (3¹/₃ lb) carrots
680 g (1¹/₂ lb) muscatel raisins
15 g (1 tbsp) tartaric acid
5 g (1 tsp) malic acid
680 g (1¹/₂ lb) sugar
Water to 4.5 litres (1 gal.)

5 g (1 tsp) pectin-
destroying enzyme
5 g (1 tsp) yeast nutrient
1 vitamin B_1 tablet
Bordeaux type yeast
Campden tablets or strong
sulphite solution

Activate the yeast starter bottle. See *Beetroot 1*
Sterilise all equipment as required. See *Beetroot 1*
Start records

Wash and scrub the carrots, slice them thinly and place in a
saucepan with 3 litres (5¹/₄ pints) of cold water. Boil without the
lid for 30 minutes. Strain from the pulp and leave to settle. After
24 hours siphon the clear liquid from the sediment. Wash the
raisins and chop or lightly liquidise them in the liquid, place
in a plastic bucket with the tartaric and malic acids,
pectin-destroying enzyme, yeast nutrient, vitamin B_1

tablet and the active yeast starter. Cover and ferment on the pulp for three days, keeping the fruit submerged and the bucket tightly covered. Strain, add the sugar and when dissolved pour into the demijohn and fit an airlock. Proceed as * in **Beetroot 1**.

Mature in bulk for 15 months before bottling.

PARSNIP 1

2 kg (4¹/₂ lb) parsnips
525 ml (19 fl oz) pineapple juice
525 ml (19 fl oz) white grape juice
5 g (1 tsp) malic acid
5 g (1 tsp) tartaric acid
2.5 g (¹/₂ tsp) grape tannin
800 g (1³/₄ lb) sugar
Water to 4.5 litres (1 gal.)

5 g (1 tsp) pectin-destroying enzyme
5 g (1 tsp) yeast nutrient
1 vitamin B₁ tablet
Bordeaux type yeast
Campden tablets or strong sulphite solution

Activate the yeast starter bottle. See *Beetroot 1*
Sterilise all equipment as required. See *Beetroot 1*
Start records

Wash and scrub the parsnips, slice them thinly and place in a saucepan with 2.5 litres (4¹/₂ pints) of cold water and gently boil for 30 minutes without the lid. Strain the pulp and leave to settle. After 24 hours siphon the clear liquid from the sediment. Add the grape and pineapple juice, malic acid, tartaric acid, grape tannin, pectin-destroying enzyme, yeast nutrient and vitamin B₁ tablet. Stir well and add the yeast starter and pour into the demijohn. Fit the airlock. When the fermentation is active, add the sugar, which should be dissolved in some of the fermenting must. Replace airlock and proceed as * in **Beetroot 1**.

Mature in bulk for 12 months before bottling.

PARSNIP 2

2 kg (4¹/₂ lb) parsnips
2 ripe bananas
1 litre (1³/₄ pints) white grape juice
250 ml (9 fl oz) elderflowers or rose petals
10 g (2 tsp) tartaric acid
3 g grape tannin
900 g (2 lb) sugar
Water to 4.5 litres (1 gal.)

5 g (1 tsp) pectin-destroying enzyme
5 g (1 tsp) yeast nutrient
1 vitamin B₁ tablet
Sauternes type yeast
Campden tablets or strong sulphite solution

Activate the yeast starter bottle. See *Beetroot 1*
Sterilise all equipment as required. See *Beetroot 1*
Start records

Wash and scrub the parsnips and cut them into small chunks. Skin the bananas, slice them and place in a saucepan with the parsnips in 2 litres (3¹/₂ pints) of cold water. Gently boil for 30 minutes with the lid off. Strain from the pulp and leave the liquid to settle. After 24 hours siphon the clear liquid from the sediment. Add the grape juice, tartaric acid, grape tannin, pectin-destroying enzyme, yeast nutrient and vitamin B₁ tablet. Stir and pour into a demijohn. Add the active yeast starter and plug the top of the jar with cotton wool. When the fermentation is active, dissolve the sugar in 750 ml (1¹⁄₃ pints) of water and add to the demijohn. Drop in the crushed flower petals and fit an airlock. Proceed as * in **Beetroot 1**. Remove the petals after three or four days.

Mature in bulk for 12 months before bottling. The wine will improve if left with a little residual sugar.

PARSNIP WITH HERBS

2 kg (4¹⁄₂ lb) parsnips
1 litre (1³⁄₄ pints) apple juice
10 g (2 tsp) tartaric acid
2.5 g (¹⁄₂ tsp) grape tannin
500 ml (18 fl oz) sweet basil leaves
5 g (1 tsp) coriander seed
900 g (2 lb) sugar
Water to 4.5 litres (1 gal.)

5 g (1 tsp) pectin-destroying enzyme
5 g (1 tsp) yeast nutrient
1 vitamin B₁ tablet
All purpose wine yeast
Campden tablets or strong sulphite solution

Activate the yeast starter bottle. See *Beetroot 1*
Sterilise all equipment as required. See *Beetroot 1*
Start records

Wash and scrub the parsnips and cut them into small chunks, place them in a saucepan with 2.5 litres (4¹⁄₂ pints) of cold water. Boil gently for 30 minutes without the lid. Strain from the pulp and leave to settle. After 24 hours siphon the clear liquid from the sediment. Add the apple juice, tartaric acid, grape tannin, pectin-destroying enzyme, yeast nutrient and vitamin B₁ tablet. Stir and pour into the demijohn with the active yeast starter. Plug the top with cotton wool. When the fermentation is active add the sugar, which should be dissolved in some of the fermenting, must, and fit an airlock. After the initial vigorous fermentation, pick the basil, crush it and put with the coriander seeds in a small nylon bag. Tie the top with a piece of cotton, leaving long ends to suspend the bag in the wine. Each day remove the airlock and give the cotton attachment a few jerks to distribute the flavour. After five days, or when enough flavour for your taste has been extracted, take out the bag and proceed as * in **Beetroot 1**.

Mature in bulk for 12 months before bottling.

SPARKLING WINES

A S YOU BECOME MORE EXPERIENCED in making your own wines, new vistas will open up and eventually you will want to explore the possibility of making sparkling wines.

Certain ingredients are more suitable for sparkling wines than others: the flavour of the fruits should not be too dominant and the acidity must be fairly high. The most suitable fruits (other than grapes, of course) are gooseberries, white currants and apples. An attractive pink 'champagne' can be made with redcurrants or sloes.

The wine is made in the normal way by extracting the fruit juices and fermenting out completely. When the fermentation has ceased, the clearing wine is siphoned from the lees into a sterile jar, but only a small quantity of sulphite is added – either 1 Campden tablet or 5 ml (1 tsp) of strong sulphite solution. Great care is needed in racking to prevent oxidation. When the wine is clear (after about 6 months) it should be racked from any sediment and prepared for the secondary fermentation. The procedure is described fully in the first recipe that follows.

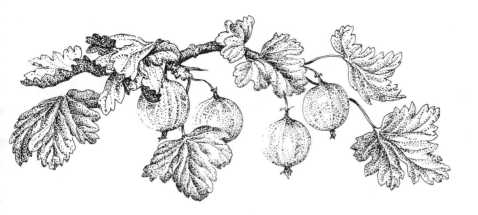

Gooseberry sparkling wine

Sulphite for sterilising: Dissolve 8 Campden tablets or 14 g sodium or potassium metabisulphite in 1 litre (1³/₄ pints) of water and store in a screw-topped bottle.

Strong sulphite solution: Add 28 g (1 oz) sodium or potassium metabisulphite to 500 ml (18 fl oz) of water. Store in a screw-topped bottle.

Yeast starter bottle: Sterilise a small bottle either by boiling for 5 minutes or filling with sterilising sulphite and leave for 20 minutes. Pour back into the storage bottle and rinse twice to remove any sulphite solution. Half fill the bottle with cooled boiled water, add the juice from half a lemon (approx. 25 ml), 10 g (2 tsp) granulated sugar and the wine yeast. Shake the bottle, plug with cotton wool and leave in a warm place, 18–21 °C (65–70 °F), for 48 hours.

1.25 kg (2³/₄ lb) gooseberries	10 g (2 tsp) pectin-destroying enzyme
453 g (1 lb) white sultanas	5 g (1 tsp) yeast nutrient
800 g (1³/₄ lb) sugar	1 vitamin B₁ tablet
Water to 4.5 litres (1 gal.)	Champagne type yeast
	Campden tablets or strong sulphite solution

Activate the yeast starter bottle
Start Records

Sterilise all equipment as required. Prepare the covered plastic bucket and utensils by washing thoroughly with warm water. Place the utensils to be used in the bucket: pour in the sterilising solution. Replace lid tightly and swirl the solution around, making sure that it reaches all parts of the bucket. Leave for 20 minutes (longer if possible) before returning the solution to the storage bottle. It will remain effective for quite a long while, providing it retains its pungent odour. Carefully wash the bucket and utensils with tap water to remove all traces of sulphite before use.

Dissolve 1 crushed Campden tablet or 5 ml (1 tsp) of strong sulphite solution in 2.5 litres (4¹/₂ pints) of cold water. Wash the gooseberries and sultanas and crush or lightly liquidise using some of the 2.5 litres (4¹/₂ pints) of water. Place in the fermentation bucket with the pectin-destroying enzyme, yeast nutrient and vitamin B_1 tablet. Stir, cover and leave for 24 hours.

Make sure the yeast starter bottle is fully active before pouring it carefully into one side of the bucket. (Retain a little in the starter bottle, half filling it again with a little cold water in case the bulk fails to activate.) If the active yeast starter is kept to a small area in the bucket, an active colony should quickly become established, at which point it can be stirred into the bulk.

When the fermentation is fully active the fruit particles will be pushed to the surface by the force of the carbon dioxide being released. A sterilised plate similar in diameter to the surface of the fermenting must should be turned upside down on top to exclude the oxygen and keep the fruit particles submerged.

Break up the cap two or three times daily, replacing the lid again as quickly as possible. After three days strain off the liquid and pour into the fermentation jar, dissolve the sugar in 1 litre (1¾ pints) of water and add.
*Fit an airlock and top up the jar with a little water after a few days. Keep in a warm place until fermentation ceases. Rack carefully and add 1 Campden tablet or 5 ml (1 tsp) strong sulphite solution.

Rack once more during the 6 months' storage period before starting the second fermentation. For this you will need a champagne yeast, activated in 142 ml (5 fl oz) of the wine and the same amount of water, with 28 ml (1 fl oz) lemon juice, 10 g (2 tsp) of sugar, a pinch of yeast nutrient and 1 vitamin B_1 tablet.

It is of paramount importance to use heavy champagne-type bottles for all sparkling wines, as considerable pressure will be built up inside them. In

heavy botle for sparkling wine

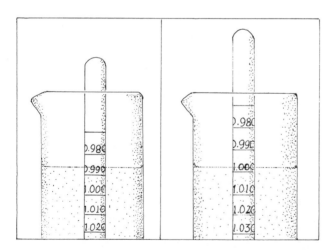

check SG reading
(preferably 0.988–0.990)

after addition of sugar,
SG 0.998

order to obtain the correct amount of carbon dioxide in each bottle, great care must be taken over the quantity of sugar used. Too little will give only a half-hearted pop when the bottle is opened and the wine will be flat; if too much is used, the cork will fly half way across the room and most of the wine will explode over the floor. The quantity of sugar used should be 85–113 g (3–4 oz) per gallon. First make sure the still wine has fermented to a specific gravity of 0.988 or 0.990. If this is the reading, 112 g (4 oz) of sugar may now be added; if the SG is 0.993, add only 70 g (2$\frac{1}{2}$ oz) (see page 147 for scale). The SG reading must not exceed 1.000, preferably 0.998. Sweeten the bulk wine with the necessary sugar; this is best done by taking out a little wine, dissolving the sugar in it and returning it to the bulk. When the champagne yeast starter is active, add it to the bulk and fix an airlock. Leave in a warm place of 18 °C (65 °F) and as soon as there is a slight release of carbon dioxide bubbles from the airlock, transfer the wine into sterile bottles, filling to within 6cm (2$\frac{1}{2}$in.) of the top of the bottle. Seal with hollow plastic sparkling wine stoppers and fix the wire cages. The bottles should be placed upside down in a crate and the crate placed in a position half way between horizontal and vertical. It is better for the temperature during the first few days to be about 13 °C (55 °F), increasing to 18 °C (65 °F).

wire cage

As the secondary fermentation progresses, a slight sediment will start forming on the side of the bottle, so each day the bottles should be given a short sharp twist, which will gradually move the sediment down into the domed stopper. After a month, most of the sediment should have settled. To make sure all the sediment is inside the hollow stopper, adjust the crate gradually, still giving the bottles a sharp twist twice weekly, until finally the bottles are vertical. The wine should be left on this small quantity of sediment for 12 months to acquire the distinctive flavour that is characteristic of good champagne.

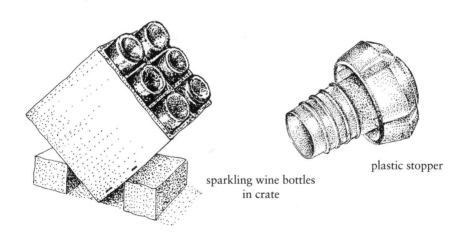

sparkling wine bottles
in crate

plastic stopper

An alternative method

Some winemakers experience difficulty in obtaining the secondary fermentation, and it is worth trying an unorthodox method which often proves successful. In this method the ingredients for the must are prepared by extracting the juices by steeping in cold water or using a juice extractor. In order to reduce the quantity of sediment, 1 g of bentonite per gallon is added to the must; it is then left for 24 hours to settle before the clear liquid is racked off and the champagne yeast starter added. The wine is fermented in a warm place and when the SG drops to 0.998, is racked into a clean jar and topped up with a little cold water. It should then be removed to a cooler place (about 10 °C, 50 °F) for 24 hours to slow down the fermentation. The wine will clear slightly as the haze subsides to the bottom of the jar. It must be racked again and the SG adjusted to 0.998, when it should be poured into prepared sterile champagne bottles to within 5cm (2in.) of the top. The procedure for storing and turning is as described above, though with this method a much larger deposit for sediment will form in the hollow domed stopper and the period needed for it to settle out will be longer, so the bottles will probably need turning for an extra month. After six to twelve months the wine will be ready for disgorgement.

Disgorgement

It is necessary to remove the sediment settled inside the hollow stopper without losing the wine. Before disgorgement the temperature of the wine should be lowered to 5 °C (40 °F) to reduce the pressure in the bottles, retaining as much carbon dioxide as possible. Care must also be taken to handle the bottles carefully so as not to disturb the sediment. In order to remove the sediment plug, the neck needs to be frozen by immersing it in a subfreezing bath, for approximately 20 minutes, either

a) by using 200 g (7 oz) crushed ice and 70 g (2½ oz) common salt, or

b) two parts of crushed ice and one part methylated spirit

The first bottle is carefully taken and turned with the stopper at approximately 45 degrees from upright. Remove the wire and then the stopper; the gas pressure will push the ice plug out with the sediment. Quickly place your thumb over the top of the bottle before topping up with a little wine or preferably a little sugar syrup to prevent the sparkling wine from being unpleasantly tart. Quickly insert a solid stopper and fit a new wire.

The question arises as to why this sugar dosage does not re-ferment? The wine has already gone through two fermentations, which will deplete nutrients other than the sugar, and with an essential 12 months ageing period and alcohol levels over 10%, the yeast cells, if any remain, have little chance to start a third fermentation.

It is not costly to make a good sparkling wine but time and patience is necessary. Some winemakers may feel it is not essential to leave the wine 12 months during the bottle fermentation and may be tempted to carry out disgorgement at 6 months. However, viable yeast may be present and if the wine is stored in a relatively warm temperature, there is a risk of another fermentation if sugar has been added. The only safe preventative measure then is to add sulphur dioxide with the sugar syrup, but these wines will not achieve the same quality.

The wines will be ready to drink after a few weeks.

APPLE AND PEAR SPARKLING WINE

1.5 kg (3¹/₃ lb) mixed apples
1.5 kg (3¹/₃ lb) pears
453 g (1lb) white sultanas
50 ml (2 fl oz) lemon juice
A few lightly scented rose petals
680 g (1¹/₂ lb) sugar
Water to 4.5 litres (1 gal.)

10 g (2 tsp) pectin-destroying enzyme
5 g (1 tsp) yeast nutrient
1 vitamin B₁ tablet
Champagne type yeast
Campden tablets or strong sulphite solution

Wash the apples and pears, and place in the freezer for 48 hours.

Activate the yeast starter bottle. See *Gooseberry sparkling wine*
Sterilise all equipment as required. See *Gooseberry sparkling wine*
Start records

Dissolve 1 crushed Campden tablet or 5 ml (1 tsp) of strong sulphite solution in 3 litres (6³/₄ pints) of cold water, add the lemon juice and the crushed, frozen apples and pears. Wash the sultanas thoroughly, chop and add with the pectin-destroying enzyme, yeast nutrient and vitamin B₁ tablet. Stir well, cover and leave for 24 hours. Add the active yeast starter and when the must is fully activated pick the rose petals, crush and add to the must. Ferment on the pulp for two or three days, keeping the fruit pulp submerged. Strain, pressing the pulp, add the sugar and when dissolved, pour into the demijohn. Proceed as * in **Gooseberry sparkling wine.**

APRICOT SPARKLING WINE

2.5 kg (5¹/₂ lb) fresh apricots **or**
2 kg (4¹/₂ lb) 'ready to eat' apricots
1 litre (1³/₄ pints) grape juice
680 g (1¹/₂ lb) sugar
Water to 4.5 litres (1 gal.)

5 g (1 tsp) pectin-destroying enzyme
5 g (1 tsp) yeast nutrient
1 vitamin B₁ tablet
Champagne style yeast
Campden tablets or strong sulphite solution

Activate the yeast starter bottle. See *Gooseberry sparkling wine*
Sterilise all equipment as required. See *Gooseberry sparkling wine*
Start records

Wash the apricots; if fresh ones are used, remove the stones. Chop them finely and place in the fermentation bucket with 1 crushed Campden tablet or 5 ml (1 tsp) of strong sulphite solution with 2.5 litres (4¹/₂ pints) of water. Add the grape juice, pectin-destroying enzyme, yeast nutrient and vitamin B₁ tablet. Stir well, cover and leave for 24 hours before adding the active yeast starter. Ferment on the pulp for three days, keeping the fruit submerged with an upturned dinner plate, stirring two or three times daily. Strain, pressing the pulp lightly, add the sugar and when dissolved pour into a demijohn and fit an airlock. Proceed as * in **Gooseberry sparkling wine.**

GRAPE SPARKLING WINE

4.5 kg (10 lb) imported white grapes
1 litre (1³/4 pints) apple juice
10 g (2 tsp) malic acid
453 g (1 lb) sugar
Water to 4.5 litres (1 gal.)

10 g (2 tsp) pectin-destroying enzyme
Champagne type yeast
Campden tablets or strong sulphite
solution

Activate the yeast starter bottle. See *Gooseberry sparkling wine*
Sterilise all equipment as required. See *Gooseberry sparkling wine*
Start records

Crush the grapes or lightly liquidise them in the apple juice without
breaking the seeds, add the malic acid and 1 crushed Campden
tablet or 5 ml (1 tsp) of strong sulphite solution and the pectin-
destroying enzyme. Cover the fruit and leave for 24 hours. Add the
active yeast starter and ferment on the pulp for two days, keeping
the fruit submerged at all times. Strain and press the pulp, add the
sugar and when dissolved pour into the demijohn. Proceed as * in
Gooseberry sparkling wine.

PINEAPPLE
AND GRAPE SPARKLING WINE

2 litres (3¹/2 pints) white grape juice
1 litre (1³/4 pints) pineapple juice
3 ripe bananas
5 g (1 tsp) malic acid
453 g (1lb) sugar
Water to 4.5 litres (1 gal.)

5 g (1 tsp) pectin-destroying enzyme
5 g (1 tsp) yeast nutrient
1 vitamin B₁ tablet
Champagne type yeast
Campden tablets or strong
sulphite solution

Activate the yeast starter bottle. See *Gooseberry sparkling wine*
Sterilise all equipment as required. See *Gooseberry sparkling wine*
Start records

Pour the grape and pineapple juice into a bucket. Peel the bananas, slice them
thinly and boil in 1 litre (1³/4 pints) of water for 20 minutes. Strain the liquid
into the juices and add the malic acid, pectin-destroying enzyme, yeast nutrient
and vitamin B₁ tablet. Stir well and pour into the demijohn, adding the active
yeast starter. Plug the top with cotton wool and when the fermentation is
active pour enough must into a jug to dissolve the sugar, returning it to the
demijohn. Fit airlock. Proceed as * in **Gooseberry sparkling wine.**

SWEET SPARKLING WINE

1 kg (2¹/₄ lb) gooseberries and white currants (or fresh apricots)
1 kg (2¹/₄ lb) dessert apples
1 litre (1³/₄ pints) white grape juice
250 ml (¹/₂ pint) elderflowers
560 g (1¹/₄ lb) sugar
Water to 4.5 litres (1 gal.)

10 g (2 tsp) pectin-destroying enzyme
5 g (1 tsp) yeast nutrient
1 vitamin B₁ tablet
Champagne type yeast
Campden tablets or strong sulphite solution

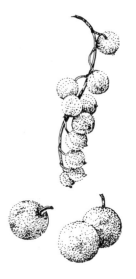

Activate the yeast starter bottle. See *Gooseberry sparkling wine*
Sterilise all equipment as required. See *Gooseberry sparkling wine*
Start records

Place the gooseberries, white currants and apples in the freezer for 48 hours. Remove and place in a bucket, pouring 2 litres (3¹/₂ pints) of near boiling water over them. As soon as they thaw, crush the fruit by hand and add the pectin-destroying enzyme, yeast nutrient, white grape juice and vitamin B₁ tablet. Stir well and pour the active yeast starter carefully into one side of the bucket, then cover. The following day the fermentation should be active. Add the flower petals and ferment on the pulp for three days, keeping the fruit submerged and stirring twice daily to break up the fruit cap. Strain, pressing the pulp lightly, and add the sugar. When the sugar has dissolved, pour into the demijohn and proceed as * in **Gooseberry sparkling wine.**

To make a sugar syrup to sweeten the wine, dissolve 453 g (1 lb) of sugar in 568 ml (1 pint) water; heat until dissolved and cool. Proceed as in Disgorgement. Check the bottles periodically, if this is your first effort, to make sure there is no sediment building up in the bottle. The wine should remain crystal clear. If in doubt, use the wine about a month after sweetening.

PINK SPARKLING WINE

680 g (1¹/₂ lb) sloes
1 kg (2¹/₄ lb) redcurrants
568 ml (1 pint) rosé grape concentrate
340 g (12 oz) sugar
Water to 4.5 litres (1 gal.)

5 g (1 tsp) pectin-destroying enzyme
5 g (1 tsp) yeast nutrient
1 vitamin B₁ tablet
Champagne type yeast
Campden tablets or strong sulphite solution

Activate the yeast starter bottle. See *Gooseberry sparkling wine*
Sterilise all equipment as required. See *Gooseberry sparkling wine*
Start records

Crush the sloes without breaking the stones or freeze for 24 hours and place in a fermentation bucket with 3 litres (6³/₄ pints) of cold water and half a crushed Campden tablet or 2.5 ml (¹/₂ tsp) of strong sulphite solution, the pectin-destroying enzyme, yeast nutrient and vitamin B₁ tablet. Cover and leave for 24 hours before adding the active yeast starter. Ferment on the pulp for two days, keeping the fruit pulp submerged. Strain, adding the grape concentrate and sugar, and when dissolved, pour into the demijohn. Proceed as * in **Gooseberry sparkling wine.** This wine is sometimes a little harsh and may be improved by the addition of a sugar syrup as in **Sweet sparkling wine.**

DESSERT WINES

THE OPPORTUNITY OF TASTING the great commercial unfortified dessert wines of the world comes very rarely to most of us: the rich smooth flavour and characteristic bouquet and aroma of the German Auslese and Trockenbeerenauslese and French Sauternes are not equalled in any other wines. The quantity of such wines produced is very limited and is only achieved when conditions are favourable for the bacterial mould Botrytis cinerea to attack the grapes as they become nearly ripe. This mould has the beneficial effect of puncturing the grape skin, absorbing a little of the water and enabling some of the remainder to evaporate. The resulting condensed grape juice has a very high concentration of sugar, often double the normal quantity. The acid content is also greater, and owing to the density of the must the fermentation is slower and stops before all the residual sugar is used. The grape crop, of course, is considerably reduced, often by as much as two-thirds the normal yield.

The home winemaker cannot hope to make wines of this quality, but very acceptable dessert wine can be made provided that the following important factors are borne in mind:

1 it is vital to obtain as much sugar as possible from the fruits;
2 extra fruits will ensure higher acid levels, sugar, flavour and body;
3 the fermenting yeast will have to tolerate a higher degree of alcohol;
4 the sulphur dioxide content will be greater, as sulphite will be tied with sugars, acids and aldehydes, forming bisulphite compounds;
5 sorbic acid will prevent secondary fermentation where there is residual sugar in a low alcohol wine (see page 15).

In order to balance acids and flavours, multiple ingredients have been selected for the following recipes. The most favoured for dessert wines are apricots, apples, ripe gooseberries, damsons, loganberries, raspberries and sloes. To create more body to the wines, bananas, pears and sultanas have been included in many of the recipes and also give the opportunity to make some all fruit juice wines, which will prove more labour saving with good results.

Pulp fermentation will extract more natural sugar, acids and nutrients from the fruits but should not exceed more than three days for white wines but red wines will need a little longer.

White dessert wines will need storing for one to two years before bottling, and reds about two to three years to reach their peak.

Apricot dessert wine 1

Sulphite for sterilising: Dissolve 8 Campden tablets or 14 g (¹/₂oz) sodium or potassium metabisulphite in 1 litre (1³/₄ pints) of water and store in a screw-topped bottle.

Strong sulphite solution: Add 28 g (1 oz) sodium or potassium metabisulphite to 500 ml (18 fl oz) water. Store in a small screw-topped bottle.

Yeast starter bottle: Sterilise a small bottle either by boiling for 5 minutes or filling with sterilising sulphite and leaving for 20 minutes. Pour back into the storage bottle and rinse twice with cold water. Half fill the bottle with cool boiled water, add the juice from half a lemon (approx. 25ml), 10 g (2 tsp) of granulated sugar and the wine yeast. Shake the bottle, plug with cotton wool and leave in a warm place, 18–21 °C (65–70 °F), for 48 hours.

1.5 kg (3¹/₃ lb) fresh apricots	10 g (2 tsp) pectin-destroying enzyme
1 kg (2¹/₄ lb) white sultanas	5 g (1 tsp) yeast nutrient
4 ripe bananas	1 vitamin B₁ tablet
Sugar	Sauternes type yeast
Water to 4.5 litres (1 gal.)	Campden tablets or strong sulphite solution

Activate the yeast starter bottle

Start records

Sterilise all equipment as required. Prepare the covered plastic bucket and utensils by washing thoroughly with warm water. Place the utensils to be used in the bucket: pour in the sterilising solution. Replace lid tightly and swirl the solution around, making sure that it reaches all parts of the bucket. Leave for 20 minutes (longer if possible) before returning the solution to the storage bottle. It will remain effective for quite a long while, providing it retains its pungent odour. Carefully wash the bucket and utensils with tap water to remove all traces of sulphite before use.

Dissolve 1 Campden tablet or 5 ml (1 tsp) of strong sulphite solution in 2.5 litres (4¹/₂ pints) of cold water. Chop the apricots finely, wash the sultanas thoroughly to remove the edible oils and chop, placing them all in a fermentation bucket. Thinly slice the peeled bananas and boil in 500 ml (18 fl oz) of water for 20 minutes. When cool, strain off the liquid into the must, discarding the pulp. Add the pectin-destroying enzyme, yeast nutrient and vitamin B₁ tablet. Stir, cover and leave for 24 hours. Add the active yeast starter, and when the fermentation starts and a fruit cap forms, cover the surface with an upturned plate to keep the pulp submerged and exclude the oxygen. Break up the cap with the plate two or three times daily.

STAGE 1: After three days strain the liquid through a nylon straining bag, pressing the pulp slightly. When the liquid or must is strained from the pulp take a hydrometer reading and increase the specific gravity to 1.070 with sugar syrup (see page 19). Pour the must into a demijohn; the jar should not be more than three-quarters full at this stage to allow for extra sugar to be added at a later date. Fit an airlock and stand the demijohn in a warm place, 18–21 °C (65–70 °F).

STAGE 2: Check the SG reading after one week and when it drops to 1.005, increase to an SG reading of 1.015 by adding sugar syrup (see page 89). Each time the SG drops, increase to 1.015 until fermentation ceases. To ensure the wine clears quickly it will be necessary to add a fining agent; use either bentonite or a simple and effective wine clearing kit (see pages 25–27 on Clearing). Move the demijohn to a cool place. After three days siphon off the wine from the lees, adding 3 crushed Campden tablets or 15 ml (1 tbsp) of strong sulphite solution. The wine can be left at an SG of 1.015 or can be increased at a later date to 1.020, according to your preference. If necessary, top up the demijohn with a little wine and replace airlock. The wine will need racking again after two weeks, with the addition of 2 crushed Campden tablets or 10 ml (2 tsp) strong sulphite solution. Rack again when necessary.

In order to protect this sweet wine from secondary fermentation it is advisable to add 560 mg sorbic acid (a small level teaspoonful) and 2 crushed Campden tablets or 10 ml (2 tsp) of strong sulphite solution, dissolved in a little wine, to the bulk.

Mature in bulk for 12 months before bottling.

APRICOT DESSERT WINE 2

453 g (1 lb) 'ready to eat' apricots
680 g (1 1/2lb) white sultanas
4 ripe bananas
1.5k g (3 1/3 b) dessert apples
100ml (3 1/2 oz) lemon juice
Sugar
Water to 4.5 litres (1 gal.)

10 g (2 tsp) pectin-destroying enzyme
5 g (1 tsp) yeast nutrient
1 vitamin B$_1$ tablet
Sauternes type yeast
Campden tablets or strong sulphite solution

Activate the yeast starter bottle. See *Apricot dessert wine 1*
Sterilise all equipment as required. See *Apricot dessert wine 1*
Start records

Wash the apples and place in the deep freezer for 48 hours. Remove and put into the plastic bucket. Pour 2 litres (3 1/2 pints) of near boiling water over the apples, and as they thaw, crush by hand. Thinly slice the peeled bananas and boil in 1 litre (1 3/4 pints) of water for 20 minutes. Strain off the liquid into the apples. Add the washed and chopped sultanas and apricots, 1 crushed Campden tablet or 5 ml (1 tsp) of strong sulphite solution, the lemon juice, pectin-destroying enzyme, yeast nutrient and vitamin B$_1$ tablet. Stir, cover and leave for 24 hours. Add the active yeast starter and when the fermentation starts and a fruit cap forms, cover the surface with an upturned plate. Break up the cap two or three times daily. Proceed as in **Apricot dessert wine 1, Stages 1 and 2**.

Mature in bulk for one year before bottling.

APRICOT DESSERT WINE 3

2 tins apricots (400 g)
1 kg (2¹/₄ lb) pears
1 kg (2¹/₄ lb) dessert apples
1 litre (1³/₄ pints) grape juice
10 g (2 tsp) tartaric acid
Sugar
Water to 4.5 litres (1 gal.)

10 g (2 tsp) pectin-destroying enzyme
5 g (1 tsp) yeast nutrient
1 vitamin B₁ tablet
Sauternes type yeast
Campden tablets or strong sulphite
solution

Activate the yeast starter bottle. See *Apricot dessert wine 1*
Sterilise all equipment as required. See *Apricot dessert wine 1*
Start records

Place the pears and apples in the deep freezer for 48 hours. When frozen remove the apples and pears and place in the fermentation bucket. Pour over 2 litres (3¹/₂ pints) of near boiling water and when cold crush the fruit by hand. Add 1 crushed Campden tablet or 5 ml (1 tsp) of strong sulphite solution, the chopped apricots and juice, tartaric acid, pectin-destroying enzyme, yeast nutrient and vitamin B₁ tablet. Cover and leave for 24 hours before adding the active yeast starter. Ferment on the pulp for three days, keeping the fruit cap submerged, and stir twice daily. Proceed as in **Apricot dessert wine 1, Stages 1 and 2.**

APPLE DESSERT WINE

2 litres (3¹/₂ pints) apple juice
1 litre (1³/₄ pints) grape juice
4 ripe bananas
500 ml (18 fl oz) cream rose petals
60 ml (4 tbsp) lemon juice
Sugar
Water to 4.5 litres

10 g (2 tsp) pectin-destroying enzyme
5 g (1 tsp) yeast nutrient
1 vitamin B₁ tablet
Sauternes type yeast
Campden tablets or strong sulphite
solution

Activate the yeast starter bottle. See *Apricot dessert wine 1*
Sterilise all equipment as required. See *Apricot dessert wine 1*
Start records

Thinly slice the bananas and boil in 500 ml (18 fl oz) of water for 20 minutes; strain the liquid into the bucket, add the apple and grape juice, the lemon juice, pectin-destroying enzyme, yeast nutrient, vitamin B₁ tablet and the active yeast starter. Pour into the demijohn and plug the top with cotton wool. After 24 hours replace the cotton wool with an airlock. When the fermentation is active, pick the flower petals and place in a nylon bag. Tie the top with a piece of cotton, leaving the ends to suspend the bag in the wine. Each day remove the airlock and give the bag a few jerks to distribute the flavour. Remove the bag after approximately five days and add 800 ml (1 pint 8¹/₂ fl oz) of sugar syrup (see page 19).

Proceed as in **Apricot dessert wine 1, Stage 2**

BLACKBERRY DESSERT WINE

1 kg (2^1/$_4$ lb) blackberries
1 kg (2^1/$_4$ lb) sloes or 700 g (1^1/$_2$ lb)
 blackcurrants
1 kg (2^1/$_4$ lb) pears
1 litre (1^3/$_4$ pints) grape juice
Sugar
Water to 4.5 litres (1 gal.)

10 g (2 tsp) pectin-destroying enzyme
5 g (1 tsp) yeast nutrient
1 vitamin B$_1$ tablet
Port or Madeira type yeast
Campden tablets or strong sulphite
solution

Activate the yeast starter bottle. See *Apricot dessert wine 1*
Sterilise all equipment as required. See *Apricot dessert wine 1*
Start records

De-stalk and wash the blackberries, the sloes and pears, crush the fruit, add
1 crushed Campden tablet or 5 ml (1 tsp) strong sulphite solution, the grape
juice and 1.5 litres (2^3/$_4$ pints) of water, the pectin-destroying enzyme, yeast
nutrient and vitamin B$_1$ tablet. Stir well, cover with an upturned dinner plate
and replace lid. Stir two or three times daily for three days before straining
off the liquid and pressing the pulp. Add the active yeast starter and pour
into the fermentation jar. Plug with cotton wool for 24 hours before replacing with an airlock. When the fermentation is active add 800 ml (1 pint
8^1/$_2$ fl oz) of sugar syrup (see page 19). Proceed as in **Apricot dessert wine 1,
Stage 2**.
    Store 18 months before bottling.

BLACKCURRANT DESSERT WINE

1 litre (1 ^{3}/$_4$ pints) blackcurrant juice
2 litres (3 ^{1}/$_2$ pints) grape juice
4 ripe bananas
Sugar
Water to 4.5 litres (1 gal.)

10 g (2 tsp) pectin-destroying enzyme
5 g (1 tsp) yeast nutrient
1 vitamin B$_1$tablet
Port or Madeira type yeast
Campden tablets or strong
sulphite solution

Activate the yeast starter bottle. See *Apricot dessert wine 1*
Sterilise all equipment as required. See *Apricot dessert wine 1*
Start records

Slice the bananas thinly and boil them in 500 ml (18 fl oz) of
water for 20 minutes. Strain the liquid into a bucket, adding the
blackcurrant and grape juice, the pectin-destroying enzyme, yeast
nutrient, vitamin B$_1$ tablet and the active yeast starter. Stir well and
pour into the demijohn. Plug the top with cotton wool for 24 hours
before fitting the airlock. Stand the demijohn in a warm place and when
fermentation is active add 800 ml (1 pint 8^1/$_2$ fl oz) of sugar syrup (see
page 19). Proceed as in **Apricot dessert wine 1, Stage 2**.
    Store in bulk for 12 months before bottling.

CHERRY DESSERT WINE

1.8 kg (4 lb) black or morello cherries
568 ml (1 pint) red grape concentrate
453 g (1lb) sultanas
7 g (¼ oz) tartaric acid
Sugar
Water to 4.5 litres (1 gal.)

5 g (1 tsp) pectin-destroying enzyme
5 g (1 tsp) yeast nutrient
1 vitamin B$_1$ tablet
Port or Madeira type yeast
Campden tablets or strong sulphite
solution

Activate the yeast starter bottle. See *Apricot dessert wine 1*
Sterilise all equipment as required. See *Apricot dessert wine 1*
Start records

Wash the cherries, crush them and place in a fermentation bucket with 2.25 litres (4 pints) of cold water. Wash and chop or lightly liquidise the sultanas and add with 1 crushed Campden tablet or 5 ml (1 tsp) of strong sulphite solution, tartaric acid, pectin-destroying enzyme, yeast nutrient and vitamin B$_1$ tablet. Stir, cover and leave for 24 hours. Add the active yeast starter and ferment on the pulp for three days, keeping the fruit cap submerged. Strain, add the grape concentrate and proceed as in **Apricot dessert wine 1, Stages 1 and 2.**
  Store for two years before bottling.

Note: An 'almondy' characteristic can be achieved by cracking a few of the kernels during the initial pulp fermentation.

DAMSON DESSERT WINE

1.5 kg (3⅓ lb) damsons
1 tin (568 ml) grape concentrate
300 g (11 oz) rosehips
Sugar
Water to 4.5 litres (1 gal.)

10 g (2 tsp) pectin-destroying enzyme
5 g (1 tsp) yeast nutrient
1 vitamin B$_1$ tablet
Port or Madeira type yeast
Campden tablets or strong sulphite
solution

Activate the yeast starter bottle. See *Apricot dessert wine 1*
Sterilise all equipment as required. See *Apricot dessert wine 1*
Start records

Wash and crush the damsons and rosehips and place in a fermentation bucket with 2 litres (3½ pints) of cold water. Add 1 crushed Campden tablet or 5 ml (1 tsp) of strong sulphite solution, the pectin-destroying enzyme, yeast nutrient and vitamin B$_1$ tablet. Stir, cover and leave for 24 hours. Add the active yeast starter and ferment on the pulp for five days, keeping the fruit cap submerged. Strain, add the grape concentrate and proceed as in **Apricot dessert wine 1, Stages 1 and 2.**
  Store at least two years before bottling.

ELDERBERRY DESSERT WINE

1.5 kg (3¹/₃ lb) elderberries
453 g (1 lb) sloes or bullaces
1 tin (567 ml) red grape concentrate
3 ripe bananas
Sugar
Water to 4.5 litres (1 gal.)

5 g (1 tsp) pectin-destroying enzyme
5 g (1 tsp) yeast nutrient
1 vitamin B₁ tablet
Port or Madeira type yeast
Campden tablet or strong sulphite
solution

Activate the yeast starter bottle. See *Apricot dessert wine 1*
Sterilise all equipment as required. See *Apricot dessert wine 1*
Start records

Wash and crush the sloes or bullaces and place them in a plastic fermentation bucket with 1 litre (1³/₄ pints) of water. Skin and thinly slice the
bananas and boil in 500 ml (18 fl oz) of water for 20 minutes, straining off
the liquid into the sloes. Add 1 crushed Campden tablet or 5 ml (1 tsp) of
strong sulphite solution, the pectin-destroying enzyme, yeast nutrient and
vitamin B₁ tablet. Cover and leave for 24 hours before adding the active
yeast starter. Ferment on the pulp for two days, keeping the fruit cap submerged with an upturned dinner plate. De-stalk the elderberries, crush as
many as possible and place in a stainless steel saucepan with 1 litre (1³/₄
pints) of water. Heat to 65 °C (158 °F) and maintain this heat for 5 minutes, remove and when cold add to the must. Ferment for a further 24
hours before straining and lightly pressing the pulp. Add the grape concentrate and stir well before pouring into the demijohn. Proceed as in **Apricot
dessert wine 1, Stages 1 and 2.**
    Mature in bulk for 18 months before bottling.

GOOSEBERRY DESSERT WINE

1.5 kg (3¹/₃ lb) gooseberries
1 kg (2¹/₄ lb) pears
2 litres (3¹/₂ pints) red grape juice
Sugar
Water to 4.5 litres (1 gal.)

10 g (2 tsp) pectin-destroying enzyme
5 g (1 tsp) yeast nutrient
1 vitamin B₁ tablet
Port or Madeira type yeast
Campden tablet or strong sulphite
solution

Activate the yeast starter bottle. See *Apricot dessert wine 1*
Sterilise all equipment as required. See *Apricot dessert wine 1*
Start records

Place the gooseberries and pears in the freezer; after 48 hours remove and
place in the fermentation bucket. Pour 1.5 litres (2³/₄ pints) of near boiling
water over the fruit. As the fruit thaws it can easily be crushed by hand.
Add the grape juice, 1 crushed Campden tablet or 5 ml (1 tsp) of strong sulphite solution, the pectin-destroying enzyme, yeast nutrient, 400 g (14 oz)
sugar and vitamin B₁ tablet. Stir well and cover with an upturned dinner
plate to keep the fruit submerged. Leave for two days, stirring twice daily
before straining off the liquid and pressing the pulp. Leave to settle for 24

hours before siphoning off the clear liquid into a demijohn. Add the active yeast starter and plug the top with cotton wool. The fermentation should start within 24 hours when the cotton wool should be replaced with an air-lock. Proceed as in **Apricot dessert wine 1, Stage 2.**

Mature in bulk for 12 months before bottling.

LOGANBERRY OR RASPBERRY DESSERT WINE

1 kg (2^1/$_4$ lb) loganberries or
1.5 kg (3^1/$_3$ lb) raspberries
453 g (1 lb) pears
3 ripe bananas
2 litres (3^1/$_2$ pints) red grape juice
Sugar
Water to 4.5 litres (1 gal.)

5 g (1 tsp) pectin-destroying enzyme
5 g (1 tsp) yeast nutrient
1 vitamin B$_1$ tablet
Port or Madeira type
yeast
Campden tablet or
strong sulphite solution

Activate the yeast starter bottle. See *Apricot dessert wine 1*
Sterilise all equipment as required. See *Apricot dessert wine 1*
Start records

Crush the loganberries and pears and place them in a fermentation bucket with 2 litres (3^1/$_2$ pints) of red grape juice. Peel the bananas, slice thinly and boil in 1 litre (1^3/$_4$ pints) of water for 20 minutes, strain the liquid into the fruit pulp and when cool add 1 crushed Campden tablet or 5 ml (1 tsp) strong sulphite solution, the pectin-destroying enzyme, yeast nutrient and vitamin B$_1$ tablet. Stir well and cover with an upturned dinner plate to keep the fruit sub-merged. Replace lid. Stir twice daily for three days before strain-ing off the liquid, pressing the pulp lightly, and add 453 g (1 lb) of sugar and the active yeast starter, stir to dissolve the sugar and pour into a demijohn. Fit an airlock and move to a warm place, 18–21 °C (65–70 °F). Proceed as **Apricot dessert wine 1, Stage 2.**

Note: Raspberries can be used instead of loganberries, being very simi-lar in composition, but as they contain less acid, an extra 500 g (1 lb 1^1/$_2$ oz) should be used.

PEACH DESSERT WINE

1.5 kg (3¹/₃ lb) fresh peaches
4 ripe bananas
1 tin (568 ml) white grape concentrate
5 g (1 tsp) malic acid
5 g (1 tsp) tartaric acid
Sugar
Water to 4.5 litres (1 gal.)

10 g (2 tsp) pectin-destroying enzyme
5 g (1 tsp) malic acid
1 vitamin B₁ tablet
Sauternes or Bordeaux type yeast
Campden tablets or strong sulphite solution

Activate the yeast starter bottle. See *Apricot dessert wine 1*
Sterilise all equipment as required. See *Apricot dessert wine 1*
Start records

Peel and slice the bananas and boil in 1 litre (1³/₄ pints) of water for 20 minutes. Strain the liquid into the fermentation bucket. Wash the peaches and slice or crush them and add to the bananas' liquid with 1.5 litres (2³/₄ pints) of water. Add the pectin-destroying enzyme, yeast nutrient, vitamin B₁ tablet, malic and tartaric acids and the active yeast starter. Replace lid. After 24 hours the fermentation should be active. Stir and cover with an upturned dinner plate to keep the fruit submerged. Leave for two days, stirring the must two or three times daily. Strain into another bucket and add the grape concentrate and 400 g (14 oz) of sugar. When dissolved pour into a demijohn. Proceed as in **Apricot dessert wine 1, Stages 1 and 2.**

PEAR DESSERT WINE

2 kg (4¹/₂ lb) pears
1 kg (2¹/₄ lb) crab apples
2 litres (3¹/₂ pints) white grape juice
3 vanilla pods
Sugar
Water to 4.5 litres (1 gal.)

10 g (2 tsp) pectin-destroying enzyme
5 g (1 tsp) yeast nutrient
1 vitamin B₁ tablet
Sauternes or Bordeaux type yeast
Campden tablets or strong sulphite solution

Activate the yeast starter bottle. See *Apricot dessert wine 1*
Sterilise all equipment as required. See *Apricot dessert wine 1*
Start records

Place the pears and apples in the freezer for 24 hours. Remove and pour 1.5 litres (2³/₄ pints) of near boiling water over them, and as they thaw, crush by hand. Add the grape juice, pectin-destroying enzyme, yeast nutrient, vitamin B₁ tablet and the active yeast starter. Ferment on the pulp for three days, keeping the fruit submerged with an upturned dinner plate. Stir two or three times daily, keeping the bucket tightly covered. Strain and add 453 g (1 lb) of sugar; when dissolved pour into the demijohn. Proceed as in **Apricot dessert wine 1, Stages 1 and 2.** The vanilla pods should be infused in the demijohn for 7–10 days before removing.

Note: If crab apples are unobtainable, use 1 kg (2¹/₄ lb) mixed apples and add 10 g (2 tsp) of malic acid.

SLOE DESSERT WINE

1 kg (2¼ lb) sloes
4 ripe bananas
2 litres (3½ pints) red grape juice
Sugar
Water to 4.5 litres (1 gal.)

10 g (2 tsp) pectin-destroying enzyme
5 g (1 tsp) yeast nutrient
1 vitamin B₁ tablet
Port type yeast
Campden tablets or strong sulphite
solution

Activate the yeast starter bottle. See *Apricot dessert wine 1*
Sterilise all equipment as required. See *Apricot dessert wine 1*
Start records

Wash the sloes and place them in a saucepan with 1 litre (1¾ pints) of water.
Heat to 65 °C (150 °F), maintaining the heat for 5 minutes, and pour into the
fermentation bucket; break the skins if necessary. Slice the peeled bananas
and boil in 500 ml (18 fl oz) of water for 20 minutes, strain the liquid into the
sloes and add the red grape juice, pectin-destroying enzyme, yeast nutrient,
vitamin B₁ tablet and active yeast starter. Cover and after 24 hours stir well
and keep the fruit submerged with an upturned plate. Ferment on the pulp for
three days, breaking up the fruit cap twice daily. Strain, pressing the pulp
lightly and add 453 g (1 lb) of sugar. When dissolved pour into a demijohn
and stand in a warm place. Proceed as in **Apricot dessert wine 1, Stage 2.**
   Mature in bulk for 18 months before bottling.

STRAWBERRY DESSERT WINE

1.5 kg (3⅓ lb) strawberries
500 g (1lb 1½ oz) gooseberries
1 kg (2½ lb) white sultanas
Sugar
5 g (1 tsp) malic acid
Water to 4.5 litres (1 gal.)

10 g (2 tsp) pectin-destroying enzyme
5 g (1 tsp) yeast nutrient
1 vitamin B₁ tablet
Port or Madeira type yeast
Campden tablets or strong sulphite
solution

Activate the yeast starter bottle. See *Apricot dessert wine 1*
Sterilise all equipment as required. See *Apricot dessert wine 1*
Start records

Wash the sultanas thoroughly, chop or lightly liquidise, to break the skins,
in 2.5 litres (4½ pints) of water and place in the fermentation bucket.
Crush the strawberries and gooseberries and add to the sultanas with the
malic acid, pectin-destroying enzyme, yeast nutrient, vitamin B₁ tablet
and 1 crushed Campden tablet or 5 ml (1 tsp) strong sulphite solution.
Stir well, cover and leave for 24 hours. Add the active yeast starter and ferment on the pulp for three days, breaking up the fruit cap twice daily. Keep
covered. Strain and proceed as in **Apricot dessert wine 1, Stages 1 and 2.**
   Mature in bulk for 12 months before bottling.

Note: If redcurrants are available, this would compliment the wine rather
than gooseberries.

GRAPES

GROWING, DEVELOPMENT AND CARE

A S YOU GAIN CONFIDENCE in making country wines, you will probably wish to try your hand at grape wines and will therefore look at the possibilities of growing your own grapes. Vines have been grown successfully in greenhouses and out of doors in southern parts of Great Britain over many centuries. Most houses with a garden will have an area suitable for growing a few vines in the open or a greenhouse large enough to take one or two.

If you plan to grow vines in the open, you must give careful consideration to choosing the most suitable site. The first point to remember is that the vine is a worshipper of the sun; this obviously presents problems for the British grower, but much can be done to make certain that your vines get the best of any sun that is available. Against a wall is an ideal site, as the wall will shelter the vine and reflect vital heat. If a larger area is planned, choose a site out of the prevailing wind, preferably on a slope facing south so that the vines may benefit from the first rays of sunshine in the morning through to the last as the sun sinks in the evening. Warmth is of paramount importance but so is shelter, as cooling winds will prevent the vines' development and production. Great care must be taken, however, to ensure the site is not in a frost pocket, as this could be very damaging in late spring or early summer when the buds are bursting.

As the roots of the vine penetrate deeply into the soil and spread laterally over a large area, the soil structure is of great importance if the feeder roots are to absorb sufficient water and nutrients from the soil. They will not thrive in heavy waterlogged conditions but will remain stinted and may eventually die. Soils cannot be exchanged but they can be changed. If the only site available is of clay, this can be improved by laying drains at least 40 cm (15 in.) below the surface to remove excessive water. A mixture of straw compost, lime, peat and sand should be worked in to increase the humus content, and this will eventually help to aerate the soil. Soils consisting mainly of chalk or limestone can be improved with a generous application of humus, bone meal and potash, but vines planted in this type of soil should be grafted on specially selected root stocks grown for the purpose.

Most garden soils consist mainly of medium loam, loamy sand or gravel. These can only be described as the perfect medium in which the vine flourishes, provided that attention is paid to liming the soil when the pH drops below 6.5 and that normal levels of phosphorous are maintained. Once the vine is well established, its roots penetrate deeply into the subsoil and in the UK it will rarely suffer from drought. In the drought years of 1975–76 the whole landscape in our Devon countryside was brown except the vineyard, which stood out as a green oasis. Too much watering will produce an excessive amount of growth and the vine will need continual summer pruning.

One train of thought has been to plant the vines in pots to control the growth. Experiments have been carried out with this system: it has certainly controlled the growth of the vine but the resulting fruit was very inferior, lacking in flavour and sweetness and produced a mediocre wine. It is a well-known fact among viticulturists that the soil plays an important part in producing quality wines.

Varieties

Before planting, due consideration should be given to the pros and cons of different varieties of vine. Many new varieties of German, Alsace and French vines were introduced into this country after World War II and planted for the first time in various parts of southern England, both in gardens and commercial vineyards. As the commercial vineyards are scattered over a wide area, climatic conditions vary considerably, and many varieties that produce well in one area have failed completely in another.

The most important attribute for an outdoor vine is that it should produce good ripe wood, enabling healthy fruiting buds to be laid down and develop in the ensuing year. In order to get the best quality fruit it is important when winter pruning not to leave too many fruiting buds on the lateral canes. In a cooler climate this should not exceed more than five or six buds on each cane – this will enable the vine to ripen its fruit within a reasonable period. The vine should have a minimum of cultural faults; some vines are more susceptible to diseases than others, the most common being powdery and downy mildews and botrytis. Unless a systematic spraying programme can be carried out, it is advisable to choose varieties that have a high resistance to these diseases.

All varieties have a credit and a debit side depending on the season, so the decision must be left to the viticulturist to select which he considers most suitable for the site available.

Müller Thurgau

In the 1960s and 1970s the predominate varieties planted in the UK were Müller Thurgau and Seyval Blanc. The Müller Thurgau was one of the main varieties grown in Germany, and with the introduction of viticulture into the UK it seemed an obvious choice for widespread planting. The hotter, dryer growing season in Germany helped to ripen its canes and it did not suffer unduly from fungal attack. The grapes produced contained adequate sugar and acidity levels, making good aromatic wines. However, in the UK we are frequently subject to cooler and wetter conditions, so consequently we are more prone to fungal diseases which have to be controlled. The Müller Thurgau came into this category and in wet autumns results were disappointing.

Seyval Blanc

This variety amazed growers by its ability to withstand inclement weather, not only by setting its fruit but also in producing good hard cane and well developed fruiting buds. It regularly produces a heavy yield of grapes. The disadvantages are lower sugar levels and high acidity, and when made as a single varietal wine it can lack body and fruitiness; however, in a good sunny year it can produce a lovely fresh wine with a slightly flinty acidity.

Madeleine Angevine
A variety that has gained considerable favour in more recent years. It has adequate vigour and will produce a good crop of ripe grapes in a cool summer, taking approximately 80 days from flower set to harvest, compared with the normal 90 to 100 days for many other varieties. In hot climates the acid level may prove to be too low and should be picked earlier or blended with a higher acid variety, but in the UK this will not be a problem.

Reichensteiner
This variety proved very successful in our vineyard, producing a regular but modest crop with high sugar levels. The loose bunches of small grapes dry more quickly in wet weather and were less vulnerable to damage by botrytis. In Germany the wine has little individual character but in the UK, with our cooler climate and longer growing season, Reichensteiner evolved with more style, and when fermented at a low temperature developed a light sophisticated nose producing a delicate wine. German visitors to our vineyard were surprised at its character and quality. The vine is quite vigorous and needs regular summer pruning to keep it under control.

Riesling
The Riesling grape took pride of place a decade or so ago but it was mainly associated with Germany. In a really hot summer it produced delicately fragrant wines with a glorious racy elegance but even in Germany it is not suitable for every site. It does best on the steep slopes of the Rheingau, Mosel and Rheinpfalz but it is far too late to ripen in the UK. A few Riesling vines were planted here in 1977 but in twenty years they only twice ripened sufficiently to make any resemblance of a quality wine.

Siegerrbe
This variety looks promising prior to flowering but if the weather is cold and wet during the flowering, the chances of getting a good set is very questionable. If the flowers set well, the grapes will produce very high sugars and are ideally suited to make a dessert-type wine with a strong muscat flavour. They ripen very early so are prone to wasp damage. Other varieties suitable for the UK are Huxelrebe, Kerner and Schönburger.

Red varieties
It is difficult to grow red grape varieties successfully in the UK unless extra heat can be created by a polytunnel or the reflected heat from a walled garden. We experimented over a twelve-year period with the following varieties: Blauberger, Dornfelder, Dunkelfelder, Cabernet Sauvignon, Merlot, Pinot Noir and Triomphe d'Alsace, all with varying degrees of success. In a protected environment Merlot and Cabernet Sauvignon produced excellent wines. Pinot Noir produced a quality deep red full-bodied wine but the small bunches of grapes and a very light crop would not enable the variety to be grown commercially in the UK.

Planting

The vine will need some form of support as it matures. The type of support needed in a garden will depend on the site available. The vines can be planted and supported in rows, supported against a garden wall, or if only a restricted area is available, a Goblet-type support may be used. Many English vineyards favour planting the vines in rows and training them in what is called the Double Guyot system (see below). In this system the vines are planted 1.2 metres (4 ft) apart with 2 metres (6 ft 6 in.) between rows, but if small cultivators are used or cultivation is done by hand, the rows can be closer together, i.e. 1.5 metres (5 ft). In large vineyards to ease the work-load a system has been adopted called the High Trellis or Geneva Double Curtain, which requires a high double wire supported by 2-metre (6 ft 6 in.) T posts. The vines are trained alternatively along each wire and as the canes grow they hang down, forming a double curtain. This method eliminates all summer pruning and the grapes cannot be damaged by badgers and rabbits. As the rows need to be planted 3 metres (10 ft) apart, this system is only suitable for a large area.

Unless the vines are pot grown they should be planted in the autumn or late spring depending on the severity of the winter. Grafted vines from the Continent are usually imported in the spring, when planting should be carried out as soon as possible. Dig a hole about 30 cm (12 in.) in diameter and about 38 cm (15 in.) deep. Break up the bottom of the hole with a fork and replace about 7 cm (3 in.) of top soil. Insert a long bamboo cane, which will act as a marker and eventual support for the vine in its first two years. If the roots are longer than 15 cm (6 in.), cut them back to this length. Place the vine in the centre of the hole, fanning the roots out in all directions. If the vine has been grafted, the waxed bulge near the top should be level with the surrounding surface. Fill in the hole and firm the soil, carefully covering the graft scar with a little soil to prevent drying out or other damage during the first year.

Pruning

Vines take about three to four years to become established before they are able to bear a useful crop of grapes. The root systems may be expected to develop at the same rate as the top growth, so if the vine has failed to generate sufficient canes and leaves, the roots will also be underdeveloped. The soil nutrient and general growing conditions should be checked in the early years, and in the dormant period the canes should be pruned back to encourage the root system. A lot of patience is required in these first few years to train and develop a healthy vine that will give a potential crop for 20 to 25 years.

There are several different methods of pruning, depending on the available site and number of vines grown.

Double Guyot System

In the first year the buds will start to burst in April or early May. After a month select two of the strongest shoots and rub off the remainder. When they reach 30 cm (12 in.) again select the strongest shoot, removing the other. As the cane grows, support it by tying loosely at intervals to the bamboo cane; this will prevent damage caused by wind. This cane will provide the main stock or trunk, so it is important to remove any side shoots up to 45 cm (18 in.) from the ground. When the cane reaches 1.5 metres (5 ft) pinch off the top.

The following January or February is the best time to prune. If the cane has not made much growth, it should be pruned back to three or four buds, repeating the process of the first year. If, however, a good strong cane has been produced which is hard and thicker than a pencil, it should be cut at 38 cm (15 in.) to form the stock or trunk of the vine. This is the permanent stem which will grow in diameter each year by adding a new layer of wood. The stock or trunk plays an important part as the connecting link between the roots and fruit canes, not only in supporting them at the desired height from the ground but acting as a channel that supplies water and nutrients from the roots to the developing vine.

In the second year when the buds burst and reach a height of 15 cm (6 in.), rub off all but the two strongest near the top of the stock. As they grow, tuck them into the supporting wires. Remove any side shoots that appear on the stock or trunk. When the canes reach 1.5 metres (5 ft) pinch off the tops.

The following January select the strongest cane near the trunk, cut to 60 cm (2 ft) and tie firmly to the bottom wire. Cut the remaining cane to three buds; this will provide good strong shoots and cane near the main stock or trunk for replacement canes for the following year. As the buds burst the next spring, the shoots will grow quickly and must be tucked in between supporting wires. If the vine produces more than eight to ten flower sets per vine in this third year, remove a few bunches, otherwise all the energy will be directed into producing grapes at this early stage rather than developing a good rooting system essential for the long-term production of the vine.

Pruning in the fourth year forms the basis for all future pruning. Select two of the strongest canes near the trunk and cut them back to 60–75 cm

THE DOUBLE GUYOT SYSTEM

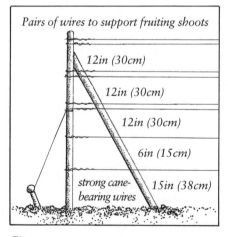

Pairs of wires to support fruiting shoots

12in (30cm)

12in (30cm)

12in (30cm)

6in (15cm)

strong cane-bearing wires   15in (38cm)

First year

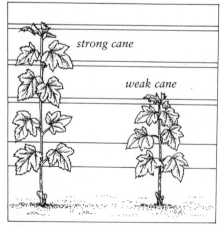

strong cane

weak cane

Following summer

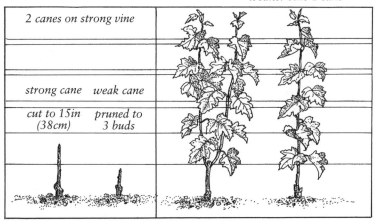

weaker vine 1 cane

2 canes on strong vine

strong cane   weak cane

cut to 15in   pruned to
(38cm)   3 buds

second year pruning   *following summer*

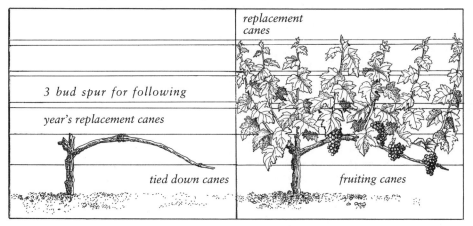

replacement
canes

3 bud spur for following

year's replacement canes

tied down canes   fruiting canes

third year pruning   *following summer*

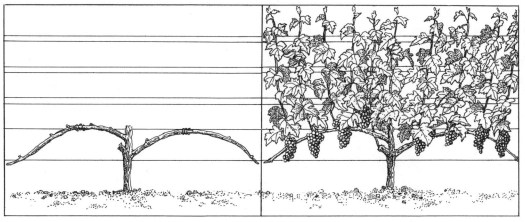

fourth year and future pruning   *following summer*

105

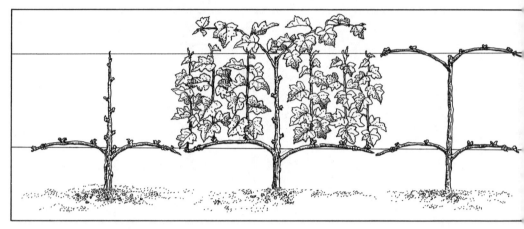

(2–2½ ft). Choose a third cane and cut it back to a three-bud spur, thus ensuring the following years' replacement canes. Remove all remaining wood and tie down the two new canes.

Horizontal cordon

Vertical and Horizontal Cordons

Vines can be grown successfully on a south-facing wall by training them as a vertical or horizontal cordon. A large expanse of brickwork on the side of a house or garden wall can be covered in different ways. Plant the vines at 3.6 metres (12ft) apart and train as in the Double Guyot System, and as they grow they can be attached to the wall forming a permanent framework. In training the vertical cordon, four or five spurs are left on the two horizontal canes that have been tied to the bottom wire. During the next summer these spurs will provide young canes from which five strong canes can be selected to form the permanent canes of the framework. They should not exceed 75cm (2½ft) in height.

Vertical cordon

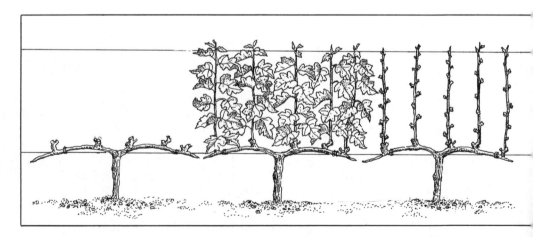

Two horizontal canes with five spurs

Growth during the following summer

Established vertical cordon with 5 or 6 spurs with fruiting buds

The following year fruit is borne on the spurs growing from these permanent canes and these should be cut back annually to three or four buds.

In training the horizontal cordon, leave two permanent canes supported by a wire at approximately 45cm (1½ft) above ground level and take a central cane near the main trunk to a higher level. This will eventually provide a permanent trunk to support another two horizontal canes at 120cm (4ft) to be tied to another wire.

It is always a temptation to leave too many fruiting buds, which will produce a mass of growth during the summer. This will be difficult to control and will encourage diseases to develop.

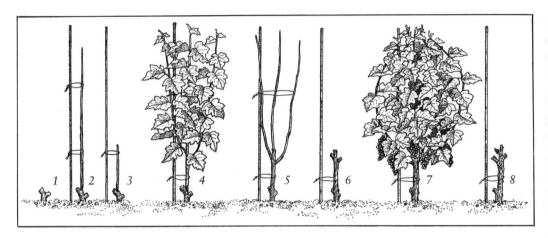

If you have only a restricted area available or want to plant a vine in odd corners of the garden, you should practise 'Head' or 'Goblet' pruning. The advantages of this method are simplicity of form and low costs. The vine is grown as in the first year of the Double Guyot system, but two three-bud spurs are left at the first pruning and four spurs the following year; these should be distributed in different parts at the head of the stock to avoid later crowding of the fruit. A 1.5 metre (5 ft) stake is erected close to the vine and the growing laterals are tied to this for support.

Head or goblet pruning

1. First year

2. End of first year

3. Prune to form permanent stick.

4. Second year's permanent growth.

5. End of second year.

6. Prune to three spurs

7. Third year's summer growth.

8. Prune to four spurs, leaving 2–3 buds on each spur

Diseases

Most of the diseases that affect the vine thrive in warm humid conditions. With a heavy rainfall in Britain we cannot escape these problems, so a spraying routine must be evolved to combat the most predominant diseases, i.e. mildews and botrytis.

Powdery mildew (Oidium)

Unlike most other fungus diseases of the grape, which are favoured by moist weather, powdery mildew thrives in warm dry weather conditions. This is identified by whitish translucent cobweb-like patches on the leaves. As the colonies develop they take on a greyish powdery appearance and a musty odour is transmitted. Flowers can be attacked so that they fail to set fruit. Large berries that are attacked develop abnormal shapes and often split or become badly scarred. The disease can be prevented by spraying with a multi-purpose systemic fungicide such as 'Spotless', which contain carbendazim and is approved under the Control of Pesticides Regulations 1986. It should be applied when the shoots are about 15 cm (6 in.) high and applied every 14 days until a month before harvest.

Botrytis

This may affect the fruit if moist and humid conditions prevail as the fruit ripens, particularly if the grapes have split or are damaged in any way. The grey mould attacks the damaged fruit, quickly spreading to the remaining berries and covering them with a mass of grey or buff-coloured spores. If the attack takes place when the grapes are nearly ripe, the affected grapes can be used to make wine even though they may look very unappetising (these are in fact the grapes which are left on the vine in Sauternes and Germany to dry out and make the lovely dessert wines). The disease should not present too great a problem and can be controlled by using a multi-purpose systemic fungicide before flowering and two weeks after flowering. It is advisable to spray again at fortnightly intervals if the weather conditions are hot and humid.

Downy mildew (Plasmopara)

The first evidence of infection is small patches of white mildew which form on the underside of the leaf. As the disease develops, the affected part of the leaf turns brown, finally becoming brittle and eventually falling off. In severely affected vines the shoots, tendrils and stems may also be attacked, which causes considerable damage to the vine. In damp weather conditions

vines growing in polythene tunnels

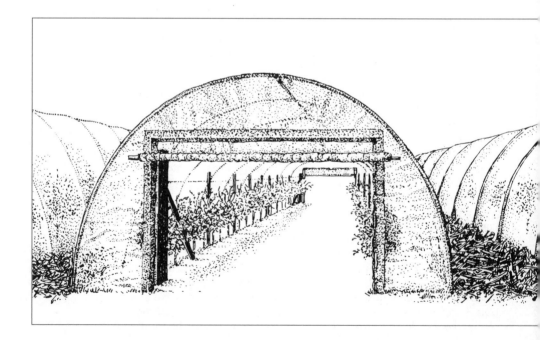

a spray of Dithane 945 or Bordeaux mixture, which contains copper sulphate, should be applied. The first application should be made just before flowering, one after flowering and another 14 days later.

Growing under cover

In good seasons vines will flourish and produce favourable crops in the open, but in adverse summers the grapes do not achieve the high sugar levels necessary for quality wines; the acid levels also remain high. In the UK when the autumn is cold and wet, malic acid will remain predominant, resulting in a harsh wine. Tartaric and malic provide 90% of the acidity in grapes, and 20 other acids make up the 10% non-nitrogenous organic acids in small quantities. During the ripening period the tartaric acid remains relatively unchanged and the drop occurs in the malic acid.

In temperatures of 21–24°C (70–75 °F) during the late summer and early autumn, enzymes can reach the berries as they ripen and break down the malic acid, and so a much softer wine is produced. In 1980 we decided to experiment in our vineyard by covering 400 of the existing vines with polytunnels. The varieties included Müller Thurgau, Reichensteiner, Huxelrebe, Scheurebe, Bacchus and Rulander. When the vines were covered they were four years old and the roots had penetrated deeply into the subsoil, so it was decided to have no irrigation within the tunnels to avoid excess humidity and condensation. A distance of 2.4 metres (8 ft) was left between each tunnel where 15 cm (6 in.) of farmyard manure was added every third year. This not only provided nutrients but acted as a sponge to retain a damp area. The vines never experienced any stress through lack of moisture, and mildews and botrytis, expected to be a major problem, were far less than suffered by those outside. None of the varieties experienced any flowering or setting problems but produced full bunches of even-sized fruit.

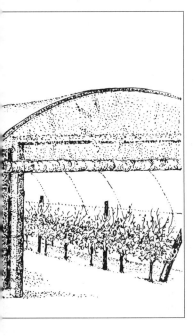

The important advantages have been the good health of the vines and the consistency of a yearly crop of good, clean fruit and ripe wood; this we attribute to the extra degree days achieved under the protection of the polytunnels.

In the parts of Germany around the Rhine and Mosel, and at Reims in France the average yearly degree days are between 900 and 1000 on the centigrade scale; below this figure the harvest is considered disastrous. In a really cold, wet summer in the UK the degree days in the open vineyard were as low as 750 compared with the polytunnels at 1100. The south-west of England is affected by a maritime climate, warmer than average in winter and spring but cooler in the summer on account of breezes coming off the sea. Vineyards in mid-south and south-east England get later bud-burst than the south-west but gain by more degree days throughout the summer and autumn. The polytunnel project has experienced few difficulties and has given winemakers an opportunity of growing grapes much further north when, even in a poor season, a regular crop of ripe grapes can be produced.

Amateur gardeners can do a great deal to protect their vines against the elements at flowering time, when a warm, dry atmosphere is necessary for the flowers to set, and during the autumn to improve ripening. This can be done by using heavy gauge polythene secured over a wooden frame propped against a wall, or, when the vines are on a trellis, by making two frames secured at the top to form an arch. The ends of the frame should remain open to allow a free flow of air, thus preventing mildew or excessive heat that could damage the vine and inhibit ripening.

Calculating degree days

Degree days are calculated by taking the mean monthly temperature above 10 °C (50 °F): this is the base-line set because no growth takes place below this temperature. The growing period is calculated over this period 1 April to 31 October.

To arrive at the mean temperature take the maximum day temperature and the minimum night temperature and divide by two. When the 'no growth' temperature of 10 °C (50 °F) has been subtracted, the figure left represents the degree days. For example:

maximum day temperature	18 °C	65 °F
minimum night temperature	10.5 °C	51 °F

mean temp. = $(18 + 10.5) \div 2 = 14.25$ °C $(65 + 51) \div 2 = 58$ °F
degree days = 14.25 °C $- 10$ °C $= 4.25$ °C 58 °F $- 50$ °F $= 8$ °F

This figure represents 4.2 degree days on the Centigrade scale and 8 degree days on the Fahrenheit scale.

Add together the daily degree days to give the monthly figure, and at the end of the season the monthly figures can be totalled to give the degree days for the season.

Commercial Vineyards

English Vineyards are no longer objects of scepticism as they were in the 1960s and 1970s. When we planted our first trial vines in 1972, visitors expected a crop within two years, but viticulture is a long-term project. The vine has to be well established with a good rooting system before cropping can commence. Traditional and new varieties were planted and tested over several years; some were not suitable for our climatic conditions, others had too many cultural problems. Certain varieties and systems of growing have evolved but this has taken time and a lot of work and expense. The formation of the United Kingdom Vineyards Association and various Regional Associations has enabled viticulturists to meet and pool their experiences in techniques and practises.

THE VINTAGE

Whether only one vine is grown or many hundreds, the romanticism of the harvest appeals to most people. It is the viticulturist alone, however, who bears the responsibility of deciding when the grapes are ready to pick. Is the specific gravity high enough or has the acid dropped to an acceptable level? Can bird and wasp damage be risked for another few days? Will the deep storm depression that is forecast completely devastate the vintage crop? All these factors must be considered in deciding when the harvest will take place. The supreme factor in making quality wine is to obtain the correct levels of sugar and acids within the fruits. It is important, therefore, to understand what occurs during the ripening period. As the fruits develop, the leaves of the vine play an important part.

The main function of the leaf is in the production of sugar for energy through the process of photosynthesis, which is the transformation of water and carbon dioxide into carbohydrate with the help of chlorophyll and in the presence of light. During the early summer the vines are growing rapidly; most of the sugars are then being used in the growth of shoots, leaves, roots and in the increase of berry size. The rapid consumption of sugars for the production of new tissues precludes any large accumulation or increase of the sugars in the berries. By the time the fruit reaches half way in its development, other active growth has slowed down or stopped and the carbohydrate materials (sugar and starch) that have accumulated in the leaves and woody parts of the vine are translocated to the fruit, where there is a rapid build-up of sugars.

Not only are we trying to achieve high sugar levels but flavour is equally important. The outer layers of the fruit, mainly in the skins, contain the greatest proportion of colouring, aroma and flavouring, and as the grape reaches maturity there is some migration of these constituents from the cell wall into the inner cell tissues. In small berried grapes there is a greater skin to pulp ratio, giving wines more aroma and flavour. This will also enhance colour and tannin in red wine.

In commercial vineyards an instrument called a refractometer is used to test the sugar content of the grapes; as the grapes vary even on the same bunch, it is essential to test several grapes from different bunches. For small-scale growers an accurate idea of the sugar content may be gained by picking a few bunches, squeezing out the juice and taking the specific gravity reading with a hydrometer.

Two or three days before picking, the yeast starter bottle should be prepared: use a cultured Mosel or Hock type yeast for white wines and a Bordeaux or Burgundy for reds. If a large quantity of grapes is to be harvested, the amount of yeast should be increased by picking some grapes and hand processing them to obtain a few gallons of juice to activate. This can be done by crushing the berries gently, placing them in a double nylon net bag and wringing the juice out by hand.

When the grapes are picked, remove them from the stalks and crush lightly, adding 1 Campden tablet or 5 ml (1 tsp) of strong sulphite solution per gallon of crushed grapes; this is important, as the juice and grapes oxidise very quickly. If a press is available, the grapes can be pressed immediately, but if they are to be hand processed, add 1 heaped teaspoon of

pectin-destroying enzyme and leave in a covered plastic bucket or container for 24 hours before pressing in a nylon bag.

An English wine should have a fresh, clean bouquet, medium dry with a specific gravity of 0.996 before bottling; this slight residual sweetness will balance the acidity, and the alcoholic content should not be more than 10.5% to 11% alcohol. In a good year some varieties of grapes will produce juice with a reading of 1.085 SG and this is the perfect medium to start the fermentation. When juice is below this SG, sugar will need to be added to increase the SG to the correct level. If you are in doubt about the acidity of the juice, or if you are making more than a few gallons, it is worth buying an acid testing kit. Most commercial English wines try to achieve an acid level of between 7.5 and 8 grams per 1000 as expressed in tartaric acid, but many kits sold in Home-made Wine and Beer shops are expressed as a percentage of sulphuric acid, so the reading would be 0.50 to 0.55 or 5 to 5.5 grams per litre. When juice exceeds this level it will need correction.

The predominant acids in grape must are tartaric and malic, with a high proportion of malic acid in poor years. Precipitated chalk is often used to neutralise some of the acid, but, as tartaric acid will be the first to be neutralised, care should be taken not to overdo the quantity used. Reducing acid in this way will be necessary in a very poor year, but it can only be described as a retrograde step and should not be practised normally. If the grapes consistently have such high acid levels, steps should be taken either to replace them with an earlier variety, or to cover them in order to increase the heat levels.

Most grapes grown in Britain are white and the juice is therefore fermented in the normal way by extracting the juice and fermenting in anaerobic conditions. When red grapes are grown for rosé or red wine, fermentation will take place on the pulp; usually three days is long enough for rosé wine, but 7 to 10 days will be necessary for the deep reds. With pulp fermentation, always keep the container tightly sealed and the fruit pulp submerged, thus ensuring a better extraction rate from the fruit and less risk of bacterial infection.

Imported grapes

Growing their own grapes and making their own wine is the ultimate achievement for most winemakers, but if they live in an area unsuitable for growing vines or in an urban environment, this may be impossible. Alternatives can be found: table grapes are imported in large quantities, and with today's speed of transport their condition on arrival is generally excellent. The wines made from table grapes will not achieve the distinctive characteristic flavour of the wine grape varieties, however, as table grapes are grown to produce large fleshy berries, which are picked as soon as they reach the minimum degree of maturity. Their development ceases as soon as they are picked and they never reach their full potential in flavour, colour or texture, so other ingredients will be needed to compensate for this lack.

Most grapes imported into Britain are from Spain or Algeria and therefore have received the optimum amount of sunshine; acidity will consequently be low and will need increasing to obtain an interesting wine. As they are picked before they reach their highest sugar potential, this will also need adjustment. It is often better to wait for a mid-season importation when the grapes will have reached a higher level of maturity. More flavour and character will be imparted to this wine if the grapes are fermented on the pulp for a few days before pressing.

Many interesting wines can be made by adding a few garden or hedgerow fruits to the grapes. For example, 340 g (^{3}/$_4$ lb) of gooseberries per gallon in white varieties will usually give the required amount of acidity and will produce a far superior wine; 225 g (^{1}/$_2$ lb) of sloes, blackcurrants or bullaces improves the insipid character of some red varieties. The winemaker thus has great opportunities to improve and enhance each year's vintage, a challenge that will provide interest and enjoyment from the moment the first fruits are gathered to the drinking of the finished product.

RECIPES

Before harvesting the grapes, take a few bunches at random, crush and squeeze out the juice and take an SG reading. If you have a large quantity of grapes, you should buy an acid testing kit, taking care to follow the accompanying instructions. The acid levels are sometimes expressed as tartaric acid, in which case 8.5 grams per litre is acceptable; if they are expressed as sulphuric acid, the reading should be 5–5.5 grams per litre.

When the levels are satisfactory you may begin to harvest, but if the acidity is too high and the SG too low, it is advisable to wait a little longer for the quality to improve.

GRAPE, WHITE

7 kg (15^1/$_2$ lb) white grapes	10 g (2 tsp) pectin-destroying enzyme
Sugar to adjust	Hock type yeast
	Campden tablets or strong sulphite solution

Activate the yeast starter bottle
Sterilise all equipment as required
Start records

It would be beneficial to hire a small press if several buckets of grapes are ready for processing, but do not remove the grapes from the stalks unless the stalks are green and sappy. Place the bunches in the press and add 10 g (2 tsp) of pectin-destroying enzyme and 1 crushed Campden tablet or 5 ml (1 tsp) of strong sulphite solution to each 7 kg (15^1/$_2$ lb) of grapes. When the juice has been extracted, leave in a large bucket with a sealed lid for 24 hours. When crushing by hand remove the grapes from the stalks and place in a plastic bucket; if the grapes are fully ripe, they can be crushed easily by hand or with a sterilised wooden block. Add the pectin-destroying enzyme and 1 crushed Campden tablet or 5 ml (1 tsp) of strong sulphite solution and stir well. Cover with an upturned plate, then cover the bucket and leave for 24 hours. Press the grapes or strain through a strong nylon straining bag, squeezing the bag to extract all the juice. Take an SG reading of the juice and adjust with sugar syrup to 1.080. Pour into a demijohn and add the active yeast starter. Plug the jar with cotton wool and when fermentation is active replace with an airlock. Leave in a warm place and before the fermentation ceases it is best to stabilise the protein. This will be achieved by adding bentonite, a form of Wyoming clay, which joins with the protein particles and which will then fall out of suspension (see pages 25–27 on Clearing). When the fermentation ceases (10–14 days), rack the clearing wine from the lees into a clean jar and remove to a cool place. After two days rack again, adding 2 Campden tablets or 10 ml (2 tsp) of strong sulphite solution and fit a cork bung. Rack again when a heavy deposit forms, adding another Campden tablet or 5 ml (1 tsp) of strong sulphite solution.

Mature in bulk for 12 months before bottling.

GRAPE, RED

7 kg (15½ lb) red grapes
Sugar to adjust

10 g (2 tsp) pectin-destroying enzyme
Burgundy or Bordeaux type yeast
Campden tablets or strong sulphite solution

Activate yeast starter bottle
Sterilise all equipment as required
Start records

Pick the grapes, remove them from the stalks and place in a plastic bucket. Crush the grapes by hand or with a sterilised wooden block. Add the pectin-destroying enzyme and 1 crushed Campden tablet or 5 ml (2 tsp) of strong sulphite solution. Stir, cover with an upturned plate, then cover the bucket and leave for 24 hours. Strain a little juice to take the SG reading and adjust with sugar syrup to 1.090. Add the active yeast starter and ferment on the pulp for 7 days, keeping the fruit submerged with the plate and the bucket tightly covered. Break up the fruit cap two or three times daily. Strain and pour into a demijohn and fit an airlock. Leave in a warm place and before the fermentation ceases it is best to stabilise the protein. This will be achieved by adding bentonite, a form of Wyoming clay, which joins with the protein particles which will then fall out of suspension (see pages 25–27 on Clearing). When fermentation ceases, rack the clearing wine from the lees into a clean jar and remove to a cool place. After two days rack again, adding 2 Campden tablets or 10 ml (2 tsp) of strong sulphite solution; fit a cork bung. Rack again when a heavy deposit forms, adding another Campden tablet or 5 ml (1 tsp) of strong sulphite solution.

Mature in bulk for 18 months before bottling.

CASKS

Suitable storage containers of glass, stainless steel and white plastic are so readily available that it does not seem prudent to revert to small oak barrels or kegs, which have the potential of turning a good wine into a disaster. Some discriminating winemakers feel it is essential for a red wine to be in contact with oak to extract tannin and allow a certain amount of ullage for the wine to develop. Barrels and kegs can harbour spoilage bacteria and allow excessive oxidation, but if the winemaker is prepared to give a great deal of time and effort to this assignment, he can be rewarded. An old cask that smells a little mouldy should never be used, but if one can be obtained that has recently been used for wine or sherry, there should not be too many problems.

The smallest size that can be safely used is 6 gallons (27 litres). The wine level will need to be checked regularly and topped up to replace the loss by evaporation. Cask storage is more suitable for red wines, as their alcoholic content is higher and they have the added protection of tannin. Storage time in small casks should be limited to six to eight months, as the ratio of cask to wine is much greater than in larger casks and the wine could become too oaky.

Each cask will develop a wine with its own characteristics and personality but often the results cannot be repeated, even following the same meticulous records. As an amateur winemaker I used cask cooperage for some red wines but the products were never identical.

When the cask is empty it should be flushed through several times with clean water before filling with 10 g (2 tsp) of sodium metabisulphite and 5 g (1 tsp) of citric acid to each litre of water. Store with the bung uppermost and knocked securely in. Before using again, check that the sulphite has retained its strong pungent smell and all will be well after flushing out with water, ready to be used again. Do not ferment in the casks, as the yeast cells will be difficult to clear. In this present age oak granules can be purchased for smaller quantities of wine and will give excellent results without so many hazards. The granules are usually from American Oak and normally, for a red wine, 3 grams to a litre of must are suspended in a small nylon bag so it can be removed after 7 to 10 days. White wines need only half the quantity of granules and need checking daily in order to achieve a slight hint of oak, or it will dominate and spoil a delicate wine.

ORGANIC WINES

T HERE WAS NO STATUTORY DEFINITION of organic food production in the UK before 1980, although there were some voluntary organic farming groups. The demand for organic food and drink escalated during the 1990s, and organic wines now command a premium of £1 to £2 per bottle. This extra cost is inevitable to pay for the considerable cost of labour and the maintenance of soil fertility involved under this system. The planting of legumes and other nitrogen-fixing plants help to increase the fertility of the soil and, together with herbs and grasses, break up the density of the soil by their root systems. Green crops and composted plant waste provide organic material and nutrient when ploughed in.

Families in many European countries often worked voluntarily part-time in their vineyards after working a full day at their agricultural or industrial employment. This self-supporting system probably accounts for their widespread organic cropping and the claim 'Italy is the Queen of Organic Production'.

The sowing of multi-mix plant species will encourage and benefit the increase of predatory insects like ladybirds, beetles, spiders, parasitic wasps and lacewings to help in controlling aphids, red spider mites and other damaging moth larvae.

There are three main fungal diseases affecting vines – they are powdery mildew, downy mildew and botrytis (blue mould). Many varieties can be affected by them, so for the production of organic wines disease resistant varieties and hybrids should be grown. Orion and Syval Blanc are ideal for the organic vineyard, and Reichensteiner and Bacchus are suitable if spray-based sulphur or copper salts are used, both of which are permitted.

Wine made from wild fruits, bullaces, blueberries, crab apples, black-berries and rosehips will be naturally organic and can be supplemented with apples, pears or bananas. Many garden fruits, gooseberries, currants and loganberries can easily be grown without artificial fertiliser or sprays, thus increasing the choice and availability of fruits.

Essential substances like sulphur dioxide and bentonite, used in conventional winemaking, are permitted in organic production along with non-organic sugar. The initial use of sulphite in the preparation of the fruit before fermentation can be limited to 25 mg per litre of must if used in conjunction with ascorbic acid at the rate of 50 mg per litre of must. The quality of the fruit needs to be good, not damaged by moulds or beginning to deteriorate. The ascorbic acid (vitamin C) will prevent oxidation of the fruit before fermentation gets underway. Ascorbic acid can be used again, with a small quantity of sulphite when the fermentation is completed; 100 mg ascorbic acid and 25 mg sulphite per litre will be sufficient during the bulk storage period.

When the wine is ready for bottling it will be necessary to add a further 100 mg ascorbic acid and 25 mg sulphite (½ Campden tablet) per litre i.e.

450 mg ascorbic acid and 100 mg sulphite per demijohn. This is the main protection for the wine against bacteria and, being a comparatively low dose, care is necessary when racking to prevent oxidation.

The alternative method of sterilising the wine is by pasteurisation. Add 50 mg ascorbic acid and 25 mg sulphite ($^1/_2$ Campden tablet) per litre i.e. 225 mg ascorbic acid and 100 mg sulphite (2 Campden tablets) per demijohn.

Tightly secure the bottles and lie them in a large, deep pan, and keep the bottles submerged in water at a temperature of 65 °C (150 °F) for 25 minutes.

ORGANIC WINE RECIPES

CRAB APPLE
(Pulp fermentation)

Sulphite for sterilising: Dissolve 8 Campden tablets or 14 g ($^1/_2$ oz) sodium or potassium metabisulphite in 1 litre ($1^3/_4$ pints) of cold water and store in a screw-topped bottle.

Strong sulphite solution: Add 28 g (1 oz) of sodium or potassium metabisulphite to 500 ml (18 fl oz) of water. Store in a screw-topped bottle.

STAGE 1: Yeast starter bottle. Sterilise a small bottle either by boiling for 10 minutes or filling with the sterilising sulphite and leaving for 20 minutes. Pour back into the storage bottle and rinse twice with cold water. Half fill the bottle with cooled boiled water, add the juice of half a lemon (approx. 25 ml), 10 ml (2 tsp) of granulated sugar and the wine yeast. Shake the bottle, plug the top with cotton wool and leave in a warm place, 18–21 °C (65–70 °F), for 48 hours.

1 kg ($2^1/_4$ lb) crab apples	10 g (2 tsp) pectin-destroying enzyme
500 g (1 lb 2oz) pears	5 g (1 tsp) yeast nutrient
500 g (1 lb 2oz) white grapes	1 vitamin B$_1$ tablet
700 g ($1^1/_2$ lb) sugar	Hock type yeast
Water to 4.5 litres (1 gal.)	Campden tablets or strong sulphite solution

STAGE 2: Sterilise all equipment as required.
Start records

Place the utensils in a white plastic bucket and pour in the sterilising solution. Replace the lid tightly and swirl the solution around, making sure that it reaches all parts of the bucket. Leave for 20 minutes, returning the solution to the storage bottle. It will remain effective for quite a long while, providing it retains its pungent odour. Carefully wash the bucket and utensils with tap water to remove all traces of sulphite.

STAGE 3: Dissolve a 200 mg vitamin C tablet (ascorbic acid) and one Campden tablet in 2.5 litres (4½ pints) of cold water. Place in the fermentation bucket with the crushed grapes and the thinly chopped or crushed crab apples and pears. Add the pectin-destroying enzyme, yeast nutrient and vitamin B₁ tablet. Stir well. Pour in the yeast starter to one side of the bucket to quickly form an active yeast colony. Cover and leave in a warm place, 18–21 °C (65–70 °F), for 24 hours, at which point the fermentation should be very active and can be stirred into the bulk. Place an upturned dinner plate on top of the fruit to keep it submerged. Break up the fruit cap twice daily for the next three days before straining off the liquid, pressing the pulp lightly, and adding 4 g of bentonite (see pages 25–27 on Clearing). Add the sugar and when dissolved pour into the demijohn and fit an airlock.

STAGE 4: Increase level in the demijohn to only seven-eighths full, as sometimes excessive frothing may occur, thus wasting the must. Replace the airlock and stand the demijohn in a warm place, 18–21 °C (65–70 °F). When the vigorous fermentation subsides, top up the demijohn with a little cold water. When the fermentation ceases (usually about two to three weeks), siphon the clearing wine from the sediment into a clean jar, top the jar up with a little cold water, replace the airlock and move to a cool place. After three days siphon off the clear wine from the sediment again, adding 450 mg ascorbic acid and 2 Campden tablets (100 mg) or 10 ml strong sulphite solution

Replace airlock. After four weeks rack again and replace the airlock with a bung. Store in a cool place for three months before bottling. Bottling can be carried out either by pasteurisation or by adding 250 mg ascorbic acid and 1 crushed Campden tablet.

BLACKCURRANT
(cold water infusion; freezing)

1 kg (2¼ lb) blackcurrants	5 g (1 tsp) pectin-destroying enzyme
600 g (1⅓ lb) red grapes	5g (1 tsp) yeast nutrient
5 ripe bananas	1 vitamin B₁ tablet
800 g (1¾ lb) sugar	Bordeaux type yeast
Water to 4.5 litres (1 gal.)	Campden tablets
	Ascorbic acid (vitamin C)

Wash the blackcurrants and grapes, removing any debris, and place in the freezer for 48 hours.

Activate the yeast starter bottle. See *Crab Apple, Stage 1*
Sterilise all the equipment as required. See *Crab Apple, Stage 2*
Start records

118

Remove the blackcurrants and grapes from the freezer and place in the plastic bucket. Pour 2 litres (3½ pints) of near boiling water over the fruit and as they thaw, crush the fruit by hand or with a flat bottomed mug. Skin the bananas, slice and boil in 1 litre (1¾ pints) of water for 20 minutes. Strain the liquid on to the fruit. Add the pectin-destroying enzyme, yeast nutrient and vitamin B$_1$ tablet. Stir well and cover the fruit with an upturned plate to keep it submerged. Replace lid and leave for three days, stirring two to three times daily, before straining. An SG reading can be taken at this stage. A reading of 1.090 will be necessary for this type of red wine. Dissolve the sugar in the must and add the yeast starter before pouring into the demijohn, fitting an airlock. Proceed as in **Crab Apple, Stage 4**.

Mature in bulk for 6 months before bottling and for 6 months in bottle.

Note: Recipes can be selected from the main sections of the book but by using organic ingredients and following the methods used in this organic section. When making a white wine it will be necessary to add 200 mg ascorbic acid (vitamin C) and 1 Campden tablet to prevent oxidation before the fermentation starts.

ELDERBERRY
(pasteurised)

1 kg (2¼ lb) elderberries	10 g (2 tsp) pectin-destroying enzyme
500 g (1 lb 2 oz) sloes or bullaces	5 g (1 tsp) yeast nutrient
4 ripe bananas	1 vitamin B$_1$ tablet
1 litre (1¾ pints) organic red grape juice	Burgundy type yeast
700 g (1½ lb) sugar	Campden tablets or strong sulphite solution
Water to 4.5 litres (1 gal.)	Ascorbic acid (vitamin C)

Activate the yeast starter bottle. See *Crab Apple, Stage 1*
Sterilise all equipment as required. See *Crab Apple, Stage 2*
Start records

Wash the elderberries and sloes and place in a large stainless steel saucepan with 1.5 litres (2¾ pints) of water. Heat to a temperature of 65 °C (150 °F) maintaining the temperature for 5 minutes. Pour into a white plastic bucket. Boil the bananas in 1 litre (1¾ pints) of water for 20 minutes and strain the liquid into the elderberries and sloe must. When cool add the grape juice, pectin-destroying enzyme, yeast nutrient and vitamin B$_1$ tablet. Stir well. Replace lid. After 24 hours, strain off the liquid, pressing the pulp. Add the active yeast starter and pour into the demijohn. Plug the top with cotton wool; this will enable the fermentation to become active when the sugar can be dissolved in the wine. Fit an airlock. Proceed as in **Crab Apple, Stage 4**.

Mature in bulk for 6 months before bottling and for 6 months in bottle.

ℒIQUEURS, COCKTAILS, FRUIT CUPS, PUNCH AND MULLED WINES

BARBECUES ARE FUN OCCASIONS, whether on a warm balmy evening when the family make a quick decision to eat outside when a couple of glasses of wine will be usually sufficient to accompany the meal; or when the occasion is a gathering for family and friends and a good punch immediately creates a party atmosphere.

Fruit or wine cups make good party starters and the main ingredients can be prepared in advance. When sparkling wine, ginger beer or lemonade are included in the recipe, these can be added just prior to serving.

When the meal is finished and guests relax, the time is ripe to serve a punch or mulled wine which helps to combat the slight chill in the air as the sun slowly sinks in the west.

Punch is a beverage introduced into England from India and so called from being usually made of five Hindu ingredients – arrack (an Eastern name for the native spirit, usually distilled from the coco-palm or from rice and sugar), tea, sugar, water and lemon juice; sometimes spices were added according to taste.

Punch is served as a chilled drink but when it is 'mulled' or warmed it is described as a mulled wine. It is essential never to boil it, as the temperature is of paramount importance. When the temperature of wine is raised about 80 °C (175 °F) alcohol will be lost in evaporation and little will be left in the wine, ruining the drink.

Mulled wines look at their best when served from a silver punch bowl, but a large stainless steel or Pyrex glass bowl can be used – even a large china mixing bowl or soup tureen is suitable. The host can create a certain amount of mystique by serving the potent tipple with a large silver or stainless steel ladle, giving the contents a whirl before pouring it into the glass. A Paris goblet or any ordinary wine glass is suitable for the mulled wine.

Wine cups and mulled wine give an opportunity to use some wines which are lacking in character, as they can be masked by the addition of fresh lemon, oranges, herbs and a small quantity of spirits or liqueurs. In selecting the base wine it is preferable to use a heavier red when serving mainly barbecue meats, and a white wine for chicken and fish.

Temperature is equally important for cold wine cups when wines should be chilled. A few ice cubes can be added to reduce the temperature, as they are best served at 8–10 °C (45–50 °F), making a crisp, cool and refreshing drink.

Cocktails give a vision of colour and exhilaration, bringing a tantalising pitch of excitement to guests in a variety of presentations. How did it acquire this unusual name? The Americans in the nineteenth century were great consumers of iced water and very fond of mixing drinks. It is said a barmaid served a handsome soldier a drink of many colours he aptly named a 'Cocks-tail'. This is an interesting version of the origin of the cocktail, and through the years it has developed by experimentation to the varied ostentatious presentations we see today. Fruit cups are an extension of the experiment, enabling interesting and sparkling drinks to be served with a lower alcoholic content, but cocktails are generally made by the addition of liqueurs.

LIQUEURS

A liqueur is defined as an alcoholic beverage containing spirits, and has always been expensive because of the cost of the alcohol content of the spirit. Originally they were made by flavouring weak spirits with aniseed, coriander and sweet fennel seed, and sweetened with sugar. In the nineteenth century small quantities were made commercially in Estonia, and as the spirits used became more refined, fruits, particularly cherries, and the kernels of the peach and apricot were infused in the spirit. Today the range has expanded and liqueurs are produced in many countries.

The base spirit for commercial liqueurs is generally distilled from grapes, apples, malted and unmalted grain, sugar cane sap, molasses, cooked rice, cocoa beans, black cherries, aniseed, sloes or potatoes. Some impart a strong and positive character, but others are more neutral: an example is vodka, which is a good base for many fruit liqueurs.

Countries throughout the world have developed their own special liqueurs and brandies, and some of these are flavoured with almonds, aniseed, caraway, cocoa bean, coffee, honey, juniper, hazelnut, nutmeg, and herbs like thyme and mint. The most popular are made by infusing fruits in spirits, and although apricot, cherry and orange are the most well known, many other fruits are used commercially: apple, blackberry, blackcurrant, black plum, artic cloudberry, coconut, melon, peach, pear, raspberry and sloe. The alcoholic content of these liqueurs varies generally between 20% and 28% alcohol.

The method of making liqueurs has varied little through the ages. The fruit or herb is steeped in the spirit for a period of time, so that the initial flavour of the fruit is absorbed by the spirit. In some recipes the sugar is added in the initial preparation: in others after straining; but in both methods the quantity of sugar can be adjusted according to taste. A smooth finish can be achieved by adding 10–20 ml (2–4 tsp) of glycerol to each recipe.

In the nineteenth and twentieth centuries when spirits were relatively cheap, the recipe books often included a section on liqueurs. They were usually based on fruits being infused in brandy, except for sloes, which were infused in gin. The fruits used were limited and were mainly cherries and a few soft fruits such as raspberries and strawberries. The range of fruits available now is far more varied, not only from our own gardens but also from the 'Pick Your Own' Centres where the superb fruits give a much

121

wider choice. More delicate fruits are enhanced by the use of vodka as the base spirit, as it does not distract from the finer flavours of the fruit. The recipes listed in this book show some variations in making liqueurs, but other fruits can be used, so extending one's knowledge and pleasures in creating one's own special liqueur.

In order to get the best extraction rate from hard fruit, i.e. sloes, cherries, currants, apricots, etc., the juice will be extracted more quickly if they are frozen for a few days, but even with a hard-skinned frozen fruit it is advisable to prick the skin a few times before placing them in a jar for infusion.

Large glass cooking storage jars, with a cover, are ideal, but large screw topped coffee jars are suitable for small quantities. After the liqueurs have been strained and settled, they should be siphoned or racked from any sediment before bottling. Some will be ready to drink in a relatively short time, others, with a higher acid content, will need a longer period in bottle to reach perfection.

The best fruits for making liqueurs are the more acidic ones. Hard fruits like sloes, bullaces and good morello cherries will need a longer period of infusion to extract the flavour and acid, whereas with blackcurrants and loganberries the period will be much shorter, or the liqueur will become too acid. The quantity of fruit used will vary according to the amount of flavour and acid required in the recipe. Bland fruits i.e. strawberries, blackberries and sweet dessert cherries will need supplementing either with a small quantity of a bland flavoured acid fruit i.e. bullaces, gooseberries, white currants, or by using a small quantity of citric acid.

As the quantity of these softer, fleshy fruits will need to be increased in order to extract enough flavour and acid, the strength of the alcoholic content will be decreased, and this will produce a softer, more fruity liqueur of 24% to 26% alcohol.

If, however, the aim is to produce an alcoholic content of 28% or more, then small quantities of strong flavoured fruits i.e. orange, blackcurrant or loganberries, should be used, which will impart enough flavour yet maintain a high level of alcohol.

A section has been included using half spirits and half dessert wine. These recipes will produce an alcoholic content of 21% to 22% and are ideal for those who prefer a less alcoholic liqueur. They are excellent, too, in enhancing culinary desserts such as ice cream, trifles, soufflés and fresh fruit.

When using citric acid the taste can be adjusted after infusion. The quantity used will be very small and, in order to get an accurate amount, it is advisable to make up an acid solution in liquid form and store in a screw topped bottle: 5 mg citric acid (1 full tsp) dissolved in 25 ml water will give 1 g of citric acid to each 5 ml (1 tsp) of liquid.

Liqueurs made from hard, solid fruits will clear and become brilliant when left to settle for a few days, but soft pulpy fruits may be difficult to clear without some help. A small addition of one of the proprietary wine clearing kits can be very effective and will clear a haze held in suspension, depositing it in a firm layer at the bottom of the bottle, enabling the clear liqueur to be siphoned off.

122

In order to achieve a high quality liqueur the fruit must be fully ripe to impart their unique and supreme qualities.

Recipe Ratings
As all the recipes in the liqueur section have been compiled during the last 12 months, tasting panels have been arranged to ascertain their merits and appeal. Some preferred a very smooth liqueur, while others choose crispness and flavour. The star ratings summarise the average points given by members of the panels.

APRICOT LIQUEUR 1 ☆☆☆☆

340 g (³/₄ lb) fresh apricots   426 ml (15 fl oz) 40% vodka
200 g (7 oz) sugar   10 ml (2 tsp) glycerol

Wash the apricots, cut in half and remove stones, quarter the fruit and place in sterilised jar. Dissolve the sugar in the vodka and pour over the fruit with 10 ml (2 tsp) glycerol. Stir the fruit daily for one month to diffuse the fruit flavour into the spirit. Strain through a fine muslin, squeezing gently to extract as much liquid as possible. Leave to settle for 48 hours for the liqueur to clear before siphoning into small bottles. Store for a few months before drinking. The liqueur will improve if kept for over a year.

APRICOT LIQUEUR 2 ☆☆☆☆☆

200 g (7 oz) 'ready to eat' dried apricots   426 ml (15 fl oz) brandy
200 g (7 oz) sugar   10 ml (2 tsp) glycerol
100 ml (3¹/₂ oz) white wine

Wash the apricots and cut into quarters and place in sterilised jar. Dissolve the sugar in the wine and pour over the apricots and leave for 24 hours before adding the brandy and glycerol. Cover jar and stir or swirl the jar daily for one month to diffuse the fruit flavour into the spirit. After one month, strain the liquid through fine muslin, squeezing the fruit gently to extract as much liquid as possible. Leave to settle for 48 hours before siphoning the clear liquid into small bottles. Store for at least 3 months before drinking.

Bilberry, Blaeberry or Whortleberry Whisky ☆☆☆

Many moorland areas abound with wild bilberries, or blaeberries as they are known in Scotland, or whortleberries in the West Country, and one is encouraged to make a rewarding excursion on the moors to collect them. Some Garden Centres stock the Highbush Blueberry which can be successfully grown in acid soils in the garden.

426 g (15 oz) bilberries or blaeberries	175 g (6 oz) sugar
70 g (2½ oz) sloes or bullaces, **or**	426 ml (15 fl oz) whisky
5 ml (1 tsp) citric acid solution	10 ml (2 tsp) glycerol

Place the bilberries and sloes (if used) in a freezer for 24 hours. Then place in a wide-necked glass jar, dissolve the sugar in the whisky, pour over the fruit and add the glycerol. Cover the jar and stir daily for three weeks to diffuse the fruit flavour into the spirit. Strain through a fine muslin, squeezing the fruit gently to extract as much liquid as possible. Leave to settle and when clear, siphon into small bottles. Store for 4 months before drinking A softer liqueur can be made by replacing the whisky with vodka, and excluding the sloes or citric acid.

Blackcurrant Liqueur 1 ☆☆☆☆☆

170 g (6 oz) blackcurrants	426 ml (15 fl oz) gin
180 g (6 oz) sugar	20 ml (4 tsp) glycerol
80 ml (3 fl oz) water	

Strip the fruit from the stalks, freeze for a couple of days before placing in a wide-necked glass jar. Dissolve the sugar in boiling water and cool before adding the gin, pour over the fruit, cover or cork and shake or stir daily for 14 days. Strain through a fine muslin cloth and adjust sugar level to taste. Let the liqueur settle for a week before siphoning into small bottles. Store for 6 months before drinking, but a year in storage will produce a more mellow liqueur.

BLACKCURRANT LIQUEUR 2 ☆☆☆☆☆

226 g (¹/₂ lb) blackcurrants
200 g (7 oz) sugar
100 ml (3¹/₂ oz) water

426 ml (15 fl oz) vodka
20 ml (4 tsp) glycerol

Wash the fruit and place in sterilised jar. Boil the water, adding the sugar and stir until dissolved, cool slightly and pour over the blackcurrants. When cool add the vodka and glycerol to the blackcurrants, and leave in a warm place, stirring or swirling the jar daily to diffuse the fruit flavour into the spirit. After 14 days strain through a fine muslin and adjust sugar level if necessary. Let the liqueur settle for a week before siphoning into clean bottles. Store for 6 months before drinking.

BLACKBERRY WHISKY ☆☆☆☆☆

400 g (14 oz) blackberries
200 g (7 oz) sugar
426ml (15 fl oz) whisky

15 ml (1 tbsp) glycerol
5 ml (1 tsp) citric acid solution

Put alternate layers of blackberries and sugar in a wide-necked jar, and add the glycerol, citric acid and whisky. Cover the jar and leave for two days. Shake or gently stir the fruit to diffuse the fruit flavours into the spirit for the next three weeks, before straining through a fine muslin cloth, gently squeezing the fruit to extract as much liquid as possible. Return to the jar for a few days or until the liqueur is clear. Decant into small bottles and cork. Keep for 6 months before drinking.

CHERRY BRANDY 1 USING MORELLO CHERRIES ☆☆☆☆☆

The Morello cherry is the best variety to make a true cherry brandy as it contains a high level of acidity, good flavour and depth of colour. If Morellos are unobtainable, the varieties May Duke or Nabella can be successfully used.

400 g (14 oz) Morello cherries
200 g (7 oz) sugar

426 ml (15 fl oz) brandy
15 ml (1 tbsp) glycerol

Prick the cherries a few times with a pin and place in the freezer for 24 hours. Put alternate layers of cherries and sugar in a wide-necked jar, add the glycerol and brandy, and cover. Swirl or stir the fruit daily for the next four weeks to diffuse the fruit flavours into the spirits, before straining through a fine muslin cloth, squeezing the fruit gently to extract as much of the liquid as possible. Return to the jar for a few days or until the liqueur is clear. Decant into small bottles and cork. Keep for 6 months before drinking.

CHERRY BRANDY 2 USING DESSERT CHERRIES ☆☆☆☆☆

When Morello cherries are unobtainable it is possible to make interesting liqueurs with dessert cherries. Good varieties are Early River, Stella, Sunburst or Merton Bigarreau. It will be necessary, however, to increase the acidity to balance the alcohol and sweetness, or the liqueur would taste insipid and uninteresting. This can be achieved by adding 10 ml (2 tsp) of citric acid solution (see page 122) or by adding 100 g (3$^{1}/_{2}$ oz) of white currants or redcurrants.

400 g (14 oz) dessert cherries	426 ml (15 fl oz) brandy
170 g (6 oz) sugar	15 ml (1 tbsp) glycerol
10 ml (2 tsp) citric acid solution	

Prick the cherries a few times with a pin and place in the freezer for 24 hours. Put alternate layers of cherries and sugar in a wide-necked jar, add the glycerol, brandy and citric acid solution, and cover. Swirl or stir the fruit daily for the next four weeks to diffuse the fruit flavours into the spirits, before straining through a fine muslin cloth, squeezing the fruit gently to extract as much of the liquid as possible. Return to the jar for a few days or until the liqueur is clear. Decant into small bottles and cork. Keep for 6 months before drinking.

DAMSON GIN ☆☆☆☆☆

400g (14oz) damsons	426ml (15fl oz) gin
200g (7oz) sugar	20ml (4 tsp) glycerol

Wash the damsons and prick the skins a few times before placing in the freezer for 24 hours. Place the frozen damsons in a wide-necked jar. Dissolve the sugar gradually in the gin and pour over the fruit, add the glycerol and cover. Stir daily for three weeks to diffuse the flavour into the spirit. After one month strain the liquid and leave to settle for 48 hours before siphoning off the clear liquid into small bottles. Store for 6 months before drinking.

LOGANBERRY LIQUEUR ☆☆☆☆☆

200 g (7 oz) loganberries	426 ml (15 fl oz) vodka
250 g (9 oz) sugar	20 ml (4 tsp) glycerol
75 ml (5 tbsp) wine	

Put the loganberries into a wide-necked jar, dissolve the sugar in the wine and vodka and pour over the loganberries. Add the glycerol, cover the jar and stir daily for three weeks. Strain through a fine muslin cloth and leave to settle for a few days before siphoning the clear liquid into small bottles. Store for 6 months before drinking, as this liqueur improves with keeping.

ORANGE BRANDY 1 ☆☆☆☆

A liqueur for Brandy lovers!

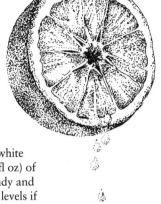

One seville orange
200 g (7 oz) sugar
112 ml (4 fl oz) water

426 ml (15 fl oz) brandy
20 ml (4 tsp) glycerol

Very thinly pare the outer rind from the orange (do not include any white pith) and place in a wide-necked jar, dissolve the sugar in 112 ml (4 fl oz) of boiling water, cool slightly and pour over the orange strips, add brandy and glycerol, and cork. Stir daily for three weeks, strain and adjust sugar levels if necessary and leave for a few days before decanting into small bottles, tightly corked. Preferably leave for 6 months before drinking.

ORANGE BRANDY 2 ☆☆☆☆

Rind from 1 seville orange
Rind from 1/4 lemon
210 g (7 1/2 oz) sugar
112 ml (4 fl oz) water
426 ml (15 fl oz) brandy

20 ml (4 tsp) glycerol
5 g (1 tsp) coriander seed
1 small cinnamon stick
Pinch of saffron

Pare the orange rind and a few strips of lemon rind very thinly (do not include any white pith). Place the rind with the coriander seed, cinnamon, saffron and glycerol in a jar. Put the sugar and water in a saucepan, bring to the boil and stir until the sugar is dissolved, then cool slightly before pouring over the orange rind with the brandy. Shake or stir the jar daily to diffuse the flavours into the spirit. After three weeks strain off the liquid and adjust sugar if necessary. Leave to settle until liqueur is clear before siphoning into clean bottles. Store for at least 6 months before drinking.

ORANGE LIQUEUR 1 ☆☆☆☆

Rind from 1 seville orange
Rind from 1/4 lemon
210 g (7 1/2 oz) sugar
112 ml (4 fl oz) water
426 ml (15 fl oz) vodka

20 ml (4 tsp) glycerol
5 g (1 tsp) coriander seed
1 small cinnamon stick
Pinch of saffron

Pare the orange rind and a few strips of lemon rind very thinly (do not include any white pith). Place the rind with the coriander seed, cinnamon, saffron and glycerol in a jar. Put the sugar and water in a saucepan, bring to the boil and stir until the sugar is dissolved, then cool slightly before pouring over the rind, and add the vodka. Shake or stir the jar daily for three weeks to diffuse the flavours into the spirit. Then strain off the liquid and adjust the sugar if necessary. Leave to settle until the liqueur is clear before siphoning into clean bottles. Store for 6 months before drinking.

Pineapple Liqueurs

Pineapples have the correct elements to make a good balanced liqueur. It is essential to procure a really ripe, golden pineapple which will give a full flavour, a high degree of sweetness and adequate acid. Prepare by slicing off the outer skin, removing any dark 'eyes' in the flesh and remove the inner hard core. Then cut into small cubes.

PINEAPPLE GIN ☆☆☆☆

450 g (1lb) pineapple
240 g (½ lb) sugar
426 ml (15 fl oz) gin
15 ml (1 tbsp) glycerol

Place the pineapple cubes in a jar. Gradually dissolve the sugar in the gin, and pour over the fruit. Add the glycerol and cover the jar. Stir once daily for the next three weeks. Strain the pineapple through a fine muslin cloth, squeezing the fruit to extract as much liquid as possible. Leave to settle for a few days before siphoning the liquid into small bottles. Store for at least 4 months.

PINEAPPLE LIQUEUR ☆☆☆☆

360 g (12½ oz) pineapple
180 g (6 oz) sugar
426 ml (15 fl oz) vodka
20 ml (4 tsp) glycerol

Proceed as for the previous recipe, using vodka instead of gin.

RASPBERRY BRANDY ☆☆☆☆

453 g (1 lb) raspberries
260 g (9 oz) sugar
426 ml (15 fl oz) brandy
10 ml (2 tsp) glycerol

Put the raspberries into a wide-necked jar, and dissolve the sugar in the brandy at normal room temperature. Pour over the raspberries and add the glycerol. Shake or gently stir the raspberries daily to diffuse the fruit flavours into the spirit. After three weeks, strain through a fine muslin cloth, squeezing to extract as much liquid as possible. Return to the bottle for a few days or until the liqueur is brilliantly clear. Decant into small bottles and cork. Store for 6 months before drinking.

REDCURRANT LIQUEUR ☆☆☆☆

350 g (12½ oz) redcurrants
250 g (9 oz) sugar
426 ml (15 fl oz) vodka
20 ml (4 tsp) glycerol

The skins of redcurrants are very firm and even when frozen often fail to split when thawed. This recipe will be enhanced if time and patience are given to pricking as many currants as possible before placing them in the freezer for 24 hours. Place the frozen redcurrants in a wide-necked jar. Dissolve the sugar in the vodka and pour over the fruit, add the glycerol and cover. Stir daily for three weeks. After one month strain the liquid, pressing the pulp lightly, and leave to settle before siphoning off the clear liquid into small bottles. Store for 6 months before drinking.

Sloe Gin ☆☆☆☆☆

600 g (1lb 1½ oz) sloes
200 g (7oz) sugar
426 ml (15 fl oz) gin

20 g (4 tsp) sweet flaked almonds
20 ml (4 tsp) glycerol

Prick the sloes several times and place in the freezer for 24 hours. Then
place them with the almonds in a clean glass jar, dissolve the sugar in the
gin at normal room temperature and pour over the fruit. Cover and leave in
a medium warm place for two months, and shake or stir the fruit each day
to circulate. Leave for another month, before straining into clean bottles
and cork securely. It may be necessary to decant after a few weeks if a sediment forms. After bottling, store for at least 6 months.

Strawberry Liqueurs

Your efforts will be well rewarded if it is possible to get enough alpine or
wild strawberries, but you will generally have to rely on summer fruiting
dessert varieties from the Pick Your Own Centres or your home-grown
ones which will need to be selected with care. The smaller fruits like Bounty
or Honeoye are ideal. These may be difficult to find, so look for medium-
sized fruit such as Bogota, Cambridge Favourite, Royal Sovereign or
Tantallon, which will impart more flavour than the very large varieties.
These dessert strawberries will need enhancing and balancing with the addition of a small quantity of acid fruit, or the addition of citric acid solution
(see page 122).

Strawberry Liqueur ☆☆☆☆

500 g (1 lb 1½oz) strawberries
150 g (5 oz) sugar
426 ml (15 fl oz) vodka

15 ml (1 tbsp) citric acid solution
10 ml (2 tsp) glycerol

Place alternate layers of strawberries and sugar in a glass jar, then add the
citric acid solution and glycerol. Cover the fruit with the vodka and after
two days shake or stir the jar daily for the next two weeks. This will help to
diffuse the fruit flavour into the spirit. Strain through a double fine muslin
cloth, squeezing the fruit, and then leave to settle before siphoning off the
clear liquid into small bottles. Store for three months before drinking.

Strawberry Brandy ☆☆☆

400 g (14 oz) strawberries
100 g (3¹/₂ oz) gooseberries
160 g (5¹/₂ oz) sugar

426 ml (15 fl oz) brandy
15 ml (1 tbsp) glycerol

It is preferable to use frozen gooseberries, slightly thawed, before pricking with a needle. Place alternate layers of strawberries, gooseberries and sugar in a glass jar, and add the glycerol. Cover with the brandy and after two days shake or stir the jar, and continue to do this for two weeks. This will help to diffuse the fruit flavours into the spirit. Strain through a double fine muslin cloth, squeezing the fruit, and then leave to settle before siphoning off the clear liquid into small bottles. After bottling, store for three months before drinking. *Note*: Redcurrants can be used as an alternative to gooseberries.

Liqueurs made with spirits and dessert wine
Making liqueurs from commercial spirits is quite expensive, and the home wine-maker can get good results by substituting part of the spirits with dessert wine of at least 14% alcohol, marrying the type of wine to the same style liqueur i.e. apricot dessert wine for apricot liqueur or a rosé for red liqueurs.

By using half spirit at 40% and half dessert wine at 14% alcohol, this will give a combined reading of 27% alcohol before the addition of fruit and sugar. When using a dessert wine of 16% this will raise the alcohol content to 28%, which, with the addition of sugar and the fruit extraction, will achieve a liqueur of 21–22% alcohol.

This level of alcohol is ideal for infusing herbs or strong-flavoured fruits such as blackcurrants, oranges or loganberries when a small volume of fruit is used. Bulky fruits with milder flavours like apricots, blackberries or pineapples will need more fruit to impart more flavour, and this will reduce the alcohol level in the liqueur, so the ratio of spirits should be increased.

Many of the liqueur recipes in the first section could be made substituting half the quantity of spirit for half dessert wine. The sugar should be dissolved in the spirit/wine base rather than in water.

Dried Apricot Liqueur using Vodka and Wine ☆☆☆☆

200 g (7 oz) 'ready to eat' apricots
200 g (7 oz) sugar
300 ml (¹/₂ pint) vodka

300 ml (¹/₂ pint) dessert white wine
5 ml (1 tbsp) glycerol

Wash and cut the apricots into quarters and place in a glass jar. Dissolve the sugar in the dessert wine and pour over the quartered apricots. Leave for 24 hours, so that the apricots absorb some of the wine, before adding the vodka and glycerol. Seal the jar and swirl or spin it daily to diffuse the fruit flavour into the spirits. After one month strain the liquid through fine muslin, squeezing the fruit to extract as much liquid as possible. Leave to settle for 48 hours before siphoning off the clear liquid into small bottles. A second siphoning may be necessary before storing for 3 months.

Blackcurrant Liqueur using Vodka and Wine ☆☆☆☆

180 g (6 oz) blackcurrants
250 g (9 oz) sugar
300 ml (1/2 pint) dessert rosé or white wine

300 ml (1/2 pint) vodka
15 ml (1 tbsp) glycerol

Place the blackcurrants in the freezer for 24 hours before putting them in a glass jar. Dissolve the sugar in the wine and vodka at normal room temperature. Pour over the currants adding the glycerol, and swirl or stir daily for two weeks to diffuse the fruit flavour into the spirits. Strain the liquid through a fine muslin, squeezing gently to extract as much liquid as possible. Leave to settle before siphoning off the clear liquid into small bottles. Store for 6 months before drinking.

Blackberry Liqueur using Vodka and Wine ☆☆☆☆

240 g (1/2 lb) blackberries
180 g (6 oz) sugar
300 ml (1/2 pint) dessert rosé
or white wine

300 ml (1/2 pint) vodka
15 ml (1 tbsp) glycerol

Place the blackberries in a glass jar and dissolve the sugar in the wine and vodka at normal room temperature. Pour over the berries adding the glycerol and swirl the jar or stir daily for two weeks to diffuse the fruit flavour into the spirits. Strain through a fine muslin, squeezing gently to extract as much liquid as possible. Leave to settle before siphoning or racking off the clear liquid. A second racking may be necessary before bottling. As there is a lack of acidity, the liqueur will be ready to drink within 3 months.

Cherry Brandy with Dessert Wine ☆☆☆☆☆

550 g (1 lb 3 1/2 oz) morello cherries **or**
550 g (1 lb 3 1/2 oz) dessert cherries with
5 ml (1 tsp) citric acid solution
300 g (11 oz) sugar

300 ml (1/2 pint) brandy
300 ml (1/2 pint) rosé or white dessert wine
10 ml (2 tsp) glycerol

Dissolve the sugar in the wine and brandy at normal room temperature. De-stalk the cherries and prick each one a few times before placing in a sterile jar. If dessert cherries are used, add 5 ml citric acid solution. Pour the liquid over the cherries and add the glycerol. Seal the jar and swirl or stir the jar daily for three weeks to diffuse the fruit flavour into the spirit. After one month strain the liquid through a fine muslin, squeezing the fruit gently to extract as much liquid as possible. Return to the jar and leave to settle for a few days before siphoning the clear liquid into small bottles. Store for 6 months before drinking.

LOGANBERRY LIQUEUR USING VODKA AND WINE ☆☆☆☆☆

250 g (9 oz) loganberries	300 ml (¹/₂ pint) dessert rosé or
250 g (9 oz) sugar	white wine
300 ml (¹/₂ pint) vodka	15 ml (1 tbsp) glycerol

Place the loganberries in a glass jar and dissolve the sugar in the wine and vodka at normal room temperature. Pour over the berries, adding the glycerol, and swirl or stir daily for two weeks to diffuse the fruit flavour into the spirits. Strain the liquid through a fine muslin, squeezing gently to extract as much liquid as possible. Leave to settle before siphoning off the clear liquid into small bottles. Store for 6 months before drinking.

ORANGE LIQUEUR USING VODKA AND WINE ☆☆☆

Outer rind of 1 Seville orange or	300 ml (¹/₂ pint) white dessert wine
from 1 orange and a few strips of	15 ml (1 tbsp) glycerol
lemon outer rind (no white pith)	5 g (1 tsp) coriander seed
200 g (7 oz) sugar	Small stick of cinnamon
300 ml (¹/₂ pint) vodka	Pinch of saffron

Place the finely shredded rind (no white pith) with the coriander seed, cinnamon, saffron and glycerol into a jar or bottle. Dissolve the sugar in the vodka and wine at normal room temperature and pour over the orange rind. Seal the jar or bottle and shake or stir daily for four weeks before straining through a fine muslin. Leave to settle in a cool place for 48 hours before decanting or siphoning into bottles.

Winemakers are generally thrifty by nature and are reluctant to throw away the fruit after straining off the liqueur, but, during the steeping period, the alcohol has extracted most of the flavour and colour from the fruit, leaving them very bland and colourless. So, although there is a temptation to use them in soufflé or other desserts, the results can be disappointing.

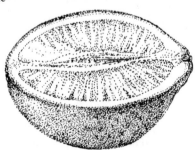

High Alcohol Kits for Making Liqueurs

In recent years new products have become available from Home-made Wine and Beer Shops for hobby wine makers who wish to widen their skills. These enable a higher alcoholic product to be made at home without distillation. The yeasts in these kits allow the fermentation to reach an alcoholic content of 21% or 37 degrees proof spirit in three weeks. All the ingredients are supplied in the kit except sugar, but wine making equipment will be required, including a 5-litre fermenting jar or demijohn, bung, airlock, siphon tube, sterilising agent and six bottles. Full and comprehensive instructions are given with each kit, and if a temperature of approximately 20 °C (68 °F) is maintained, the fermentation will be completed in three weeks, giving a hydrometer reading between 0.988 and 0.990.

The kit will make six 75 cl bottles of unflavoured basic spirit, which can form the base for adding to a Liqueur Extract or for fruit infusion. The Tasting Panels were generally agreed that the Kit liqueurs could not achieve the quality ratings of the fresh fruit with commercial spirits at 40% alcohol. The cost of making these is inevitably high, so the option of using only Kit spirits in liqueurs at a quarter of the cost is a great temptation. I have selected a few recipes using the Basic Kit Spirits infused with fresh fruit. The recipes tasted by the Judging Panel favoured the strong-flavoured fruits when the quantity of fruit used was much less and did not reduce the alcoholic content to an unacceptable level.

Liqueurs made with High Alcohol Kits and Fresh Fruit

APRICOT ☆☆

300 g (11 oz) 'ready to eat' apricots
200 g (7 oz) sugar
600 ml (1 pint) Kit spirit

10 ml (2 tsp) glycerol
10 ml (2 tsp) citric acid solution

Wash and cut the apricots into quarters and place in a glass jar. Dissolve the sugar in the Kit spirit and pour over the fruit, then add the glycerol and citric acid. Seal the jar and stir daily. After one month, strain the liquid through a fine cloth, squeezing the fruit to extract as much liquid as possible. Leave to settle and when clear siphon off the liquid into a bottle and cork. Store for 3 months before drinking.

BLACKCURRANT ☆☆

180 g (6 oz) blackcurrants
200 g (7 oz) sugar

600 ml (1 pint) Kit spirit
20 ml (4 tsp) glycerol

Wash and dry the blackcurrants and freeze for 24 hours before placing them in a wide-necked jar. Dissolve the sugar in the Kit spirit and pour over the fruit, then add the glycerol. Seal the jar and stir daily for three weeks. Strain the liquid through a fine cloth and leave to settle. When clear, siphon off the liquid into a bottle and cork. Store for 3 months before drinking.

LOGANBERRY ☆☆

226 g (¹/₂ lb) loganberries
180 g (6 oz) sugar

600 ml (1 pint) Kit spirit
15 ml (1 tbsp) glycerol

Place the loganberries in a wide-necked jar. Dissolve the sugar in the Kit spirit and pour over the fruit, then add the glycerol. Seal the jar and stir daily for three weeks. Strain the liquid through a fine cloth and leave to settle. When clear, siphon off the liquid into a bottle and cork. Store for 3 months before drinking.

SLOE ☆☆☆

500 g (1lb 1¹/₂ oz) sloes
220 g (7³/₄ oz) sugar

600 ml (1 pint) Kit spirit
20 ml (4 tsp) glycerol

Prick the sloes and place in the freezer for 24 hours before placing in a wide-necked jar. Dissolve the sugar in the Kit spirit and pour over the fruit, then add the glycerol. Seal the jar and stir daily for one month. Then leave for another month before straining through a fine cloth and leave to settle. When clear, siphon off the liquid into a bottle and cork. Store for at least 6 months, preferably 12 months.

ORANGE ☆☆

1 Seville orange
Outer rind of one orange
90 g (3 oz) sugar
300 ml (¹/₂ pint) Kit spirit

15 ml (1 tbsp) glycerol
Half a cinnamon stick
2.5 g (¹/₂ tsp) coriander seed
A pinch of saffron

Finely shred the outer rind of the orange (no white pith), peel the orange and slice diagonally (removing any white pith), and place together in a wide-necked jar. Dissolve the sugar in the Kit spirit and add, with the glycerol, cinnamon stick, coriander seed and saffron, to the fruit. Seal the jar and stir daily for three weeks before straining through a fine muslin. Leave to settle before siphoning the clear liquid into a bottle and seal. Store for 6 months before drinking.

All the above liqueurs were given a higher rating when made with two-thirds Kit spirit and one-third commercial spirit at 40% alcohol.

HIGH ALCOHOL KITS AND ESSENCES FOR MAKING LIQUEURS

The Basic Kit Spirit flavoured with Liqueur Extracts gave divided opinions within the Tasting Panel; some imparted a synthetic taste, while others were found to be acceptable. As the cost of these extracts is not excessive and new ones are appearing on the market, it is advisable to consult the Home-made Wine and Beer suppliers on new and improved products. The Tasting Panels generally agreed the imported Swedish essences gave a clean and fruity liqueur.

The extracts are usually sold in 50 ml bottles, which is sufficient to flavour two or three 75 cl bottles. Some extracts are rather overpowering, and although most of the instructions provide for two bottles, a test should be made to ascertain the strength desired. It is necessary to add sugar, which should be dissolved in the spirit, but this will reduce part of the original alcohol content from 21% to approximately 17–18%.

Simplicity is the main advantage of using extracts or essences; the utensils needed are available in the home and the time to make these liqueurs is quite minimal.

The sugar should be dissolved by putting all the ingredients into a jug and stirring periodically until the sugar has dissolved. Taste the liqueur for sweetness and acidity, and adjust, if necessary, by adding 5 ml or 10 ml (1 or 2 tsp) of citric acid solution (see page 122) before pouring into a sterile bottle, corking and labelling. It is best to leave the liqueur for at least a fortnight to enable the ingredients to homogenise.

The list of extracts that can be added to produce Liqueur types is extensive, e.g. Apricot, Apple Schnapps, Amaretto, Cherry Brandy, Coconut Rum, Crème de Menthe, Coffee Rum, Strawberry Daiquiri, Sloe Gin, and several Cream Liqueur types.

OCKTAILS

WHEN THE BASIC WINES and liqueurs have been made, there is the opportunity and pleasure of expanding into making Cocktails, Punches and Mulled Wines. These unique drinks can be made for special occasions or the odd cocktail to savour on a warm summer evening.

For the party host a standard cocktail shaker not only looks impressive but chills the ingredients of the cocktail effectively.

Half fill the shaker with whole ice cubes and the cocktail ingredients, and shake until the outside of the vessel is cold. Pour immediately through the strainer into a 14 cl or 5 fl oz cocktail glass, leaving the ice behind. If you then wish to add a few cubes of ice, a double cocktail glass of 20 cl or 7 fl oz will be required. (When a shaker is not available, whisk the ingredients with a fork in a small jug before straining into a glass.) It is advisable to use purified drinking water or a good bottled water to make ice cubes for inclusion in a cocktail.

Cocktails contain a high proportion of liqueurs, so it is necessary to be precise in measuring the ingredients.

1 single measure is 25 ml or 2.5 cl
This is more accurate than
1 measure equals 0.9fl oz

Some recipes require the addition of sugar syrup, and this can be made, bottled and stored. Dissolve equal volumes of water and sugar, simmer for one minute and cool.

136

Sweet Memories

2 measures of apricot brandy
1 measure of white wine

1 measure of pineapple juice
1/4 measure of sugar syrup

Shake and strain into a glass and decorate with pineapple or apricot slices.

Moonshine

2 measures of apricot brandy
1 3/4 measures of white wine

1/4 measure of lemon juice
1 measure of soda water

Shake and strain into a glass and decorate with mixed fruit.

Highland Fantasy

2 measures of blackberry whisky
1 1/2 measures of rosé wine

1/4 measure of lemon juice
1 measure of grape juice

Shake and strain into a glass and add a twist of lemon.

Summer Evening

2 measures of raspberry liqueur
2 measures of red grape juice

1 measure of ginger ale

Shake and strain into a glass and decorate with strips of crystallised ginger.

Happy Hour

2 measures of orange liqueur
1 measure of orange juice

1 measure of bitter lemon

Shake and strain into a glass and decorate with strips of crystallised lime and orange fruits.

Twilight Memory

1 1/2 measures of sloe gin
1 measure of loganberry liqueur

2 1/2 measure of cola

Shake and strain into a glass.

Cherry Blossom

1 measure of sparkling wine
3 measures of cherry brandy

1 measure of passion fruit juice

Shake and strain into a glass and decorate with glacé cherries or fresh cherries.

OVER THE TOP

2 measures of sparkling wine
1 measure of apricot brandy

1 measure of loganberry liqueur
1 measure of strawberry brandy

Shake and strain into a glass and decorate with sugar dipped strawberries or strips of 'ready to eat' apricots.

CELEBRATION

2 measures of sparkling wine
1 1/2 measures of orange liqueur

1 measure of raspberry liqueur
1/2 measure of orange juice

Shake and strain into a glass and decorate with a twist of orange.

SERENADE

1 1/2 measures of sparkling wine
2 1/2 measures of orange liqueur

1 measure of orange juice

Shake and strain into a glass and decorate with a sugar cube soaked in orange liqueur and a twist of orange.

SUMMER DELIGHT

2 measures of sparkling wine
2 measures of strawberry liqueur

1 measure of grapefruit juice

Shake and strain into a glass and decorate with half strawberries.

LONG DRINKS

LONG DRINKS ARE LESS ALCOHOLIC and need to be served in a 25 cl (8½ fl oz) glass i.e. tumbler or goblet, to accommodate the ice cubes and the ingredients. Long drinks can be embellished with fresh or crystallised fruits, or a paper parasol, and are often served with a straw and a cocktail stick to help procure the fruits.

WINTER SUNSHINE

2 measures of apricot brandy
2 measures of apricot dessert wine

3 measures of sparkling bitter lemon

Mix and pour over half a glass of ice cubes, decorate with green glacé cherries and a twist of lemon.

APRICOT ROSÉ

2 measures of apricot liqueur
1 measure of dessert white wine

1 measure of orange juice
3 measures of pineapple juice

Mix and pour over half a glass of ice cubes, decorate with crystallised pineapple slices and a green cherry.

BLACKBERRY COLA

2 measures of blackberry whisky
2 measures of blackberry
or damson dessert wine

3 measures of cola

Mix and pour over half a glass of ice cubes, decorate with a mixture of glacé cherries (red, green, cream).

BLACKCURRANT BANSHEE

2 measures of blackcurrant liqueur
1 measure of damson dessert wine
½ measure of sugar syrup

1½ measures of grape juice
2 measures of lemonade

Mix and pour over half a glass of crushed ice, decorate with two green glacé cherries and a twist of lemon.

CHERRY RIPE

3 measures of cherry brandy
2 measures of dessert or table white wine

1 measure of grape juice
1 measure of cherryade

Mix and pour over half a glass of ice cubes and decorate with maraschino cherries and a sprig of mint.

ROLLER COASTER

3 measures of orange liqueur
2 measures of grapefruit juice

1 measure of white grape or apple juice
1 measure of soda water

Mix and pour over half a glass of ice cubes and decorate with a twist of orange and green grapes.

PUNCH

THE RECIPES ARE DESIGNED to serve 15 wine glasses, 15 cl (5 fl oz) size. It is preferable to add one lump of ice to the punch bowl rather than ice cubes but it should be removed after the first serving in order to avoid excessive dilution.

ORANGE PUNCH

75 cl bottle of sparkling wine
20 cl (7 fl oz) of orange liqueur
40 cl (14½ fl oz) of orange juice

10 cl (3½ fl oz) of lemon juice
75 cl bottle of ginger ale

Mix all the ingredients, except the sparkling wine and ginger ale in a large jug and chill. When ready to serve pour all the ingredients with the sparkling wine and ginger ale into the punch bowl. Cut two small oranges in half and drop into the punch, adding a small block of ice.

SUMMER PUNCH

75 cl bottle of red wine
20 cl (7 fl oz) of cherry brandy or liqueur
5 cl (2 fl oz) of lemon juice

50 cl (18 fl oz) of cranberry juice
20 cl (7 fl oz) of sparkling water

Mix all the ingredients and chill before pouring into the punch bowl. Add stoned cherries, lemon slices and a small block of ice.

GINGER PUNCH

75 cl bottle of dry white wine
20 cl (7 fl oz) of orange liqueur
25 cl (9 fl oz) of grapefruit juice

25 cl (9 fl oz) of orange juice
100 cl (1¾ pints) of ginger ale

Mix all the ingredients, except the ginger ale, and chill for two hours. Add the ginger ale, strips of crystallised ginger and a small block of ice when ready to serve.

PINEAPPLE AND ORANGE PUNCH

75 cl bottle of white wine
20 cl (7 fl oz) of orange liqueur or brandy
40 cl (14½ fl oz) of pineapple juice

40 cl (14½ fl oz) of orange juice
15 g (1 tbsp) of fresh pineapple chunks
30 cl (11 fl oz) of ginger ale

Mix all the ingredients, except the pineapple chunks and ginger ale, and chill for two hours. Pour into the punch bowl with a small block of ice, the pineapple chunks, the ginger ale and a few thin slices of orange.

NON ALCOHOLIC CUPS

PINEAPPLE AND ORANGE SPARKLER

Mix equal quantities of pineapple and orange juice and ginger ale. Add a few cubes of pineapple, quarter slices of orange or mixed summer fruits.

COKA COOLER

Half fill a glass with iced cola, add 25 ml (1 fl oz) of blackcurrant puree and a few cubes of ice.

Note: To make blackcurrant puree place 60 g (2 oz) of blackcurrants in a saucepan with 20 ml (4 tsp) of water and 30 g (1 oz) of sugar. Place on low heat (but do not boil) to soften the fruit before pressing the fruit through a sieve.

RASPBERRY SURPRISE

Half fill a glass with lemonade and add 25 ml (1 fl oz) of raspberry puree, and a few ice cubes. Top up with a red grape juice and serve with a few fresh raspberries.

Note: Raspberry puree can be made as above using raspberries instead of blackcurrants.

SUMMER LEISURE

Use 3 measures of white or red grape juice, 2 measures of bitter lemon, 1 measure of ginger ale and add a few ice cubes.

MULLED WINE

(7 servings)

Remember when making mulled wine that the wine must not be boiled, as when the temperature rises above 80 °C (175 °F) alcohol will be lost by evaporation. Mulled wines have been popular since the eighteenth century when they were served mainly at Christmas time. We now serve them at barbecues, when their warming effects are most appreciated, giving a satisfying inner glow.

One recipe named 'The Bishop' was included in Dr Samuel Johnson's Dictionary in 1755. The 1755 recipe is as follows:

2 lemons, 8 cloves, 6 lumps of sugar, 1 bottle of port-type wine,
1/2 pint (284 ml) of water Prepare a moderate oven.

1   Warm a glass punch bowl and glasses by filling with hot water
     (not boiling) and leave until required.
2   Scrub the lemons, stud one lemon with cloves, place on a
     baking sheet in the centre of the oven for 30 minutes.
3   Rub sugar lumps over the skin of the other lemon and squeeze
     out the juice.
4   Place wines, sugar lumps, lemon juice, port-type wine, half
     pint of water (284 ml) and clove studded lemon into a large
     saucepan. Heat to 75 °C (165 °F) but do not boil. Pour into a
     warmed punch bowl and ladle into glasses.

MULLED RED WINE (7 servings)

1 bottle of red wine	10 cloves
50 ml (2 fl oz) raspberry or loganberry liqueur	1/4 tsp each of cinnamon and ginger
	1 lemon
284 ml (10 fl oz) of water	90 g (3 oz) of sugar

Scrub the lemon and pare very thinly from the outer rind, but do not include any white pith. Place in a saucepan with the spices, sugar and water, and bring to the boil. Simmer for ten minutes, then cool slightly. Place a tissue in a sieve and strain into a basin. Just before serving, place the wine, liqueur and spiced liquid into a saucepan and heat to 75 °C (165 °F), but do not boil. Pour into a warm serving bowl and taste, add more sugar if necessary.

FAMILY CHOICE (12 servings)

1 litre (1³/₄ pints) of red wine
50 ml (1³/₄ fl oz) of loganberry liqueur
750 ml (1¹/₃ pints) of water
¹/₄ tsp of freshly grated nutmeg

10 cloves
1 cinnamon stick
90 g (3 oz) of sugar
1 orange

Boil the water, cloves, cinnamon stick and sugar over low heat for ten minutes, cool and strain. Before serving, pour the wine, liqueur and the strained spiced liquid into a saucepan, heat to 75 °C (165 °F) but do not boil, and pour into a punch bowl. Scrub the orange and cut into thin slices and add before serving.

WINE CIRCLE FAVOURITE
(24 servings in 15 cl glasses)

2¹/₂ bottles of red wine
1 litre (1³/₄ pints) of water
10 eggs
226 g (¹/₂ lb) of sugar

2.5 g (¹/₂ tsp) each of powdered cloves, nutmeg and cinnamon
1 lemon
Orange

1   Put the spices in a saucepan with the finely peeled rind of the orange and lemon (no white pith). Add 1 litre (1³/₄ pints) of water and bring to the boil, simmer for ten minutes, cool slightly and strain.
2   Whisk the egg yolks in a large cooking bowl with half the sugar until creamy, and beat the egg whites until stiff.
3   Pour the wine and half the spiced water with the remaining sugar, into a large pan and heat until hot, but do not boil.
4   Meanwhile heat the serving bowl.
5   Fold the stiffly beaten egg whites into the egg yolks adding the remaining half of the spiced water and mix.
6   Pour the heated drink into the egg mixture, whisking vigorously to prevent the eggs from curdling but not to destroy the creamy froth. Serve immediately.

'A superb drink after a barbecue.'

CHRISTMAS QUICKIE (10 servings)

1¹/₂ bottles of red wine
150ml (¹/₄ pint) of cherry brandy
110g (¹/₄ lb) of sugar

28g (1oz) of blanched almonds
56g (2oz) of seeded raisins
56g (2oz) of glacé cherries

Slowly heat all the ingredients until quite hot but do not boil. Pour into a warm punch bowl and, when serving, ladle some of the fruit into each glass or cup.

COFFEES

THE POPULARITY OF IRISH COFFEE became apparent after World War II and was served in top class restaurants. The quantity of spirit used was one part to five parts of black coffee, sugar to taste, topped with a dessert spoon of whipped cream which was carefully floated on the top and sprinkled with chocolate powder.

Over the years innovations have gradually increased and, instead of whisky, other spirits and liqueurs are used, including Crème de Cacao, Curacao, Irish Mist, Kirsch and Tia Maria. Kahlua, a Mexican coffee liqueur, has gained popularity and gives the coffee a subtle mellowness.

The coffee recipes will require heatproof glasses, goblets or cups, and it is advisable to warm them before adding the hot coffee. Goblets will contain 20–25 cl (7–9 fl oz)and cups 15–20 cl (5–7 fl oz).

1 measure = 2.5 cl or 0.9 fl oz.

TRADITIONAL IRISH COFFEE

5 measures of hot black coffee   1 tbsp thin whipped cream
1 measure of whisky   Sugar to taste

Add whisky to coffee in a glass and sweeten to taste. Slowly float the cream on top and sprinkle with chocolate powder. In recent years Bailey's Irish Cream is often used to enhance the cup.

COFFEE DE-LUXE

5 measures of hot black coffee   1 tbsp of thin whipped cream
1 measure of orange brandy   Sugar to taste
1/2 measure of Tia Maria

Add the orange brandy and Tia Maria to the coffee and sweeten to taste. Slowly float the cream on top and grate a little crystallized orange peel on to the cream.

SWEET DREAMS

5 measures of hot black coffee
1 measure of brandy
1 measure of Kahlua

1 tbsp of thin whipped cream
Sugar to taste

Add the coffee, brandy and Kahlua to the glass and sweeten to taste. Slowly float the cream on top and sprinkle with a few crushed instant coffee granules.

MEXICAN COFFEE

5 measures of hot black coffee
1^1/$_2$ measures of Kahlua

1 tbsp of thin whipped cream
Sugar to taste

Add the coffee and Kahlua to the glass and sweeten to taste. Slowly float the cream on top and sprinkle with a little chocolate powder

PUERTO RICO

5 measures of hot black coffee
1^1/$_2$ measures of rum

1 tbsp of thin whipped cream
Sugar to taste

Add the coffee and rum to the glass and sweeten to taste. Slowly float the cream on top and sprinkle with a little ground, sweet mixed spice

BAILEY'S IRISH CREAM

5 measures of hot black coffee
2 measures of Bailey's Irish Cream

1 tbsp of thin whipped cream
Sugar to taste

Pour the black coffee into the glass, sweeten to taste and add the Bailey's Irish Cream. Slowly float the cream on top and sprinkle with a little chocolate powder.

SPECIFIC GRAVITY

WEIGHT OF SUGAR

Specific gravity	Oz per gallon	Grams per demijohn (4.545 litres)	Potential alcohol (% by volume)
1.000	0	0	0.0
1.005	2	56	0.7
1.010	4	120	1.3
1.015	6	180	1.9
1.020	8	241	2.6
1.025	11	300	3.3
1.030	13	361	4.0
1.035	15	422	4.6
1.040	17	482	5.2
1.045	19	539	5.9
1.050	21	602	6.6
1.055	24	666	7.3
1.060	25	723	7.9
1.065	28	782	8.5
1.070	30	843	9.2
1.075	32	907	9.8
1.080	34	964	10.5
1.085	36	1021	11.1
1.090	38	1084	11.8
1.095	40	1148	12.4
1.100	42	1205	13.1
1.105	44	1262	13.7
1.110	47	1325	14.4
1.115	49	1389	15.0
1.120	51	1446	15.7

TEMPERATURE

Centigrade	Fahrenheit	Pasteurisation	
4 °C	40 °F	65 °C	150 °F
7 °C	45 °F	73 °C	163 °F
10 °C	50 °F		
13 °C	55 °F		
14 °C	57 °F		
15 °C	59 °F		
16 °C	61 °F		
17 °C	62 °F		
18 °C	65 °F		
21 °C	70 °F		

ACID COMPARISON TABLES

Tartaric	Citric	Malic	Sulphuric
1.53	1.43	1.37	1.00
2.29	2.14	2.05	1.50
3.06	2.86	2.73	2.00
3.83	3.57	3.42	2.50
4.59	4.29	4.10	3.00
5.36	4.99	4.78	3.50
6.12	5.71	5.47	4.00
6.89	6.43	6.15	4.50
7.65	7.14	6.84	5.00
8.42	7.86	7.82	5.50

METRIC CONVERSION

Weight		Liquid Measures	
2.2 kg	5 lb	4.5 litres	1 gallon
1.8 kg	4 lb	2.2 litres	1/2 gallon
1.3 kg	3 lb	568 ml	1 pint
902 g	2 lb	284 ml	1/2 pint
453 g	1 lb	28 ml	1 fl oz
226 g	1/2 lb	15 ml approx.	1/2 fl oz
113 g	1/4 lb	8 ml approx.	1/4 fl oz
28 g approx.	1 oz		
14 g approx.	1/2 oz		
7 g approx.	1/4 oz		

GLOSSARY

Acid Essential in winemaking to give a strong and healthy fermentation. It gives character to the wine: too little and the wine will be flat and insipid, too much and the wine will be tart. The principal acid in ripe grapes is tartaric, whereas apples and wild blackberries contain a high proportion of malic acid; all citrus fruits, red, black and white currants contain a high proportion of citric acid.

Acetic Acid The acid of vinegar produced when alcohol is oxidised by bacteria. Tolerated quantities in wine range from 0.5 to 1 gram per litre.

Aerobic, anaerobic Aerobic fermentation takes place in the presence of oxygen and anaerobic fermentation in its absence. Wine yeast cells have the ability to live in both conditions.

Airlock A glass or plastic device forming a water trap which prevents the flow of air and airborne micro-organisms into the must while allowing the carbon dioxide produced by the fermentation to escape.

Alcohol The colourless, volatile spirit, ethyl alcohol, resulting from the fermentation of sugars into approximately equal parts of alcohol and carbon dioxide gas.

Aroma A fragrant, attractive smell derived from the ingredients of fruits and flowers used in making wine. More pronounced in young wine.

Astringency A term used to describe the unpleasant dryness in the mouth which can be caused by excessive amounts of tannin in the wine; this is not a serious flaw, for the wine will become softer and mellow with age.

Autolysis The breakdown of dead yeast cells by the enzyme systems of the yeast. The decomposition can cause off flavours in the wine if it is left for too long before racking.

Bacteria The micro-organisms of bacteria are present everywhere and both aerobic and anaerobic bacteria can affect wine. Both are inhibited in low pH wines or by heat, alcohol and sulphite. All bacterial infection can be prevented by cleanliness and by using the correct quantity of sulphite.

Balanced Must The correct proportions of acid, sugar, tannin and fruit extract gives fullness to a wine: a full-bodied wine is the opposite to a watery and thin wine.

Bentonite A fining agent consisting of natural clay which has a negative charge and is used to clear hazes caused by proteins that are positively charged.

Body A term used to describe the taste and feel of a wine in the mouth, which may be full-bodied, medium or thin.

Bouquet The pleasant smell a mature wine gives off when opened. The bouquet is attained as the wine ages by sweet smelling compounds called esters which are formed by the slow oxidation of acids and alcohol.

149

Calyx The outer part of a flower, formed of sepals.

Campden Tablets Tablets of potassium or sodium metabisulphite used, when dissolved, for sterilising equipment and for adding to musts and wine to suppress spoilage organisms.

Cap The fruit pulp which is pushed to the top of the fermenting must by carbon dioxide gas bubbles entrapped between particles of fruit. This cap must be broken up and pushed down frequently to prevent infection and to achieve a good extraction from the fruit.

Carbon dioxide The gas given off during the process of fermentation by the conversion of sugar to alcohol. Approximately half the sugar in the must is converted to carbon dioxide and half to alcohol.

Character The definite and unmistakable qualities of wine associated with taste, colour and bouquet.

Citric Acid The main acid of citrus fruits, currants and many soft fruits, e.g. raspberries, loganberries, strawberries and elderberries. It promotes a good fermentation and provides some antiseptic properties but does little to improve bouquet or flavour.

Clarification When fermentation ceases the suspended particles gravitate to the bottom of the container or jar and the wine becomes clear. A few wines will clear and be brilliant after using the recommended quantity of sulphite, but most white wines will require the use of bentonite or one of the proprietary trade-named brands of 'Wine clearing kits'.

Collodial hazes Insoluble cellulose particles can remain in suspension because their electrical charges repel each other. Wines that develop hazes after clearing may be affected by spoilage bacteria.

Demijohn A glass jar of 4.5-litre (1-gallon) capacity used for the fermentation and bulk storage of wine.

Dessert wine A sweet, full-bodied wine usually drunk at the end of a meal.

Dry wine A wine without any trace of sweetness. Most table wines contain a little residual sugar which is often masked by the degree of acidity but these are generally still classified as dry wines.

Effervescence The fizzing seen in a bottle of sparkling wine when it is opened, caused by the release of carbon dioxide bubbles.

Enzymes The conversion of sugar into alcohol requires at least a dozen enzymes in the complicated process that produces trace elements, compounds and alcohol in winemaking. They work through a whole sequence of chemical changes.

Esters Sweet smelling compounds formed during maturation of the wine by the reaction between acids and alcohol

Fermentation The process of changing must to wine: yeast enzymes convert sugar into alcohol, carbon dioxide and complex trace elements

Fining The process of clearing a cloudy wine with a substance that coagulates the particles in suspension and deposits them on the bottom of the jar.

Glycerol (Glycerine) A by-product of fermentation which confers a smoothness to the finished wine.

Harsh A wine that is coarse and astringent is described as harsh. This is mainly due to excessive tannin, and such a wine will need longer to mature.

Hydrometer An instrument used for measuring the density or thickness of a liquid in which it is floated. In winemaking it is used to measure the amount of sugar present.

Infusion The steeping of ingredients in water or wine to extract flavour and colour.

Lactic Acid A by-product of fermentation present in wine in small quantities; larger amounts result from a malo-lactic fermentation.

Lees The sediment that collect at the bottom of the fermentation jar, consisting of dead yeast cells, tartrates and other insoluble salts.

Liqueur A strong alcoholic liquid, sweetened and flavoured with fruits, herbs or spices.

Malic acid The principle acid found in apples, black, red and white currants, wild blackberries, rhubarb and unripe grapes. It helps in ester-forming reactions, which make a direct contribution to the bouquet of the wine.

Malo-lactic fermentation It converts the sharp malic acid into the softer lactic acid and carbon dioxide by the lactic acid bacteria (lactobacilli). Malo-lactic fermentation can be prevented by early and regular racking, by maintaining sulphite levels, by adequate acidity levels and by storing in a cool temperature.

Maturation The ageing period after fermentation ceases when complex chemical reactions take place. The overall effect will be a reduction in astringency as tannin combines with other compounds and precipitates out. Time is required to allow for the slow oxidation of acids and alcohol to form esters that bestow bouquet to the wine.

Mulled wine A wine which has been warmed, sweetened and spiced.

Must Fruit juice extract or pulp before fermentation is complete.

Nutrients Wine yeasts require nourishment to maintain a strong fermentation. Generally grapes contain sufficient amino acids and other forms of available nitrogen to support yeast metabolism during fermentation. In country wines an extra nitrogen source is necessary.

Oxidisation Wine naturally takes up some oxygen from the air, which is essential for its development. The quantity required is minimal, however, so careful racking at all times is important to prevent over oxidisation. While a little oxidisation may be desirable in some dessert wines, it is detrimental in table wines, where it causes a brownish tint and impairs the flavour.

Pasteurisation The raising of the temperature of the ingredients to 66 °C (150 °F) for 5 minutes to enable a quick extraction of flavour and colour and the killing of any bacteria present. To sterilise bottled wine submerge for 25 minutes at 65 °C (150 °F).

Pectin-destroying enzyme A preparation that destroys the pectin in fruits. High levels of pectin may cause a haze in the finished wine

pH A scale of numbers used to express degrees of acidity or alkalinity in solutions.

Precipitation As the wine matures, the insoluble compounds fall out of solution to form a deposit in the storage vessel.

Pulp fermentation Fermentation in the presence of fruit to extract acids, sugars, flavour, tannins, nutrients and vitamins.

Punch A beverage composed of wines or spirits with a combination of fruit juices, lemonade or ginger beer, herbs, spices and fruits.

151

Racking The siphoning of the clear wine from the sediment into an empty jar after fermentation ceases and during maturation.

Sediment The accumulation of matter that sinks to the bottom of the fermentation or wine vessel. During fermentation this deposit is often referred to as lees, and when the wine has cleared as crust or argols.

Social wine Wines which may be drunk at any time, without food. These may be medium-dry or medium-sweet according to taste. The alcoholic content is usually higher than in table wines, ranging from 10% to 14% by volume.

Sorbic acid Used in conjunction with sulphite to prevent a secondary fermentation in sweeter wines.

Specific gravity (SG) The weight of any substance or solution as compared with the weight of an equal volume of water. Water becomes more dense when sugar is added to it and its specific gravity is increased. Alcohol is less dense than water so as the sugar is converted into alcohol the specific gravity is reduced.

Stablising The prevention of refermentation in the presence of residual sugar by racking and the use of sulphite.

Stuck fermentation A fermentation that stops prematurely, often caused by excessive amounts of sugar, lack of nutrients or incorrect temperature.

Sulphite The name most often used when referring to sodium or potassium metabisulphite (Campden tablets) used in solution to sterilise equipment. It is an effective inhibitor of unwanted bacteria and yeast in must and wine.

Tannin A substance found in the skins, seeds and stalks of fruits, which, due to its astringent qualities, give character and 'bite' to the wine.

Tartaric acid The principal acid found in ripe grapes

Topping up Each time the wine is racked there is a small loss that leaves air space at the top of the storage vessel. A little water should be added to bring the liquid to within 24mm (1in.) of the bung.

Vinosity A must correctly fermented becomes a vinous wine taking on a harmonious balance of diverse substances, with the bouquet and aroma giving the final accolade.

Yeast Single-celled micro-organism, of which there are many species. The one used in winemaking is Saccharomyces cerevisiae, variety ellipsoideus, which secretes enzymes that act as catalysts in reducing sugar to alcohol and carbon dioxide.

INDEX